Athletic
Training
institute

Personal
Best
Set
Third

Athletics in
Schools and Colleges

THE LIBRARY OF EDUCATION

A Project of The Center for Applied Research in Education, Inc.

G. R. Gottschalk, Director

Categories of Coverage

I	II	III
Curriculum and Teaching	Administration, Organization, and Finance	Psychology for Educators

IV	V	VI
History, Philosophy, and Social Foundations	Professional Skills	Educational Institutions

Athletics in
Schools and Colleges

CHARLES A. BUCHER

Professor of Education
New York University

RALPH K. DUPEE, JR.

Polytechnic Preparatory Country
Day School

The Center for Applied Research in Education, Inc.
New York

LIBRARY OF CONGRESS
CATALOG CARD NO.: 65-20309

PRINTED IN THE UNITED STATES OF AMERICA

Foreword

Never before in the history of our nation has the role of sports been as important as it is today. Our society is characterized by automation, increased leisure, space exploration, scientific discovery, and tensions at home and abroad. In such a setting, school athletics can make a contribution to physical well-being, skillful performance, relaxation, and repose as well as to the inculcation of sound values. Games and contests furnish opportunities for self-discovery, self-expression, self-acceptance, and self-discipline. In sport, the circumstances of birth, color, race, and creed are transcended by performance and by deed.

The achievement of such outcomes requires effective leadership, appropriate activities, good organization, and sound policies. There must be programs for the skilled and the inept, for boys and for girls, for the old and for the young; all must be based on a sound philosophy of athletics and education.

It is to these purposes that this book is dedicated. Readers will find here both history and philosophy and will come to understand more fully the scope of school athletics. Units of competition, award systems, tournaments, and eligibility are discussed; problems of insurance, safety, subsidization, and finance are probed; intramurals, extramurals, and varsity athletics are treated; policies are presented and standards reviewed.

Dr. Bucher and Mr. Dupee have brought to bear on these topics their knowledge and deep understanding of athletics as well as their skill and experience in writing. This book will prove invaluable to the inexperienced director, helpful to the established athletic administrator, and useful as a reference for principals, superintendents, school board members and interested laymen. No library should be

v

without it and it might well serve as a supplementary book for
classes in athletic administration. Thoughtful readers and students
of athletics will be well rewarded for the hours spent in its perusal.

R. B. FROST

Buxton Professor and Director of
Health, Physical Education, and Recreation
Springfield College
President, American Association for
Health, Physical Education, and Recreation

Athletics in Schools and Colleges

Charles A. Bucher
Ralph K. Dupee, Jr.

Of the most frequently discussed facets in American education today, athletics in schools and colleges gets a large share of attention. Arguments have been presented for and against athletics, in all forms, for all students, and at all levels of instruction. This volume admirably summarizes the major issues in this area. Evidence to support views in a range of programs from intramural to intercollegiate athletics is supplied by the authors.

Opening with the historic development of athletics, the authors carry the reader skillfully through readable and practical concepts, pausing momentarily here and there, to state and discuss an issue. Logical presentations on intramural and extramural athletics, interscholastic and intercollegiate athletics, girls' and women's athletics, and athletic standards for various educational levels give comprehension to these subjects. Competition in this volume is treated wisely, with unbiased reporting of the findings of professional groups. For the reader who wants to know specific athletic program details in such areas as organizing for competition, eligibility, awards, and financing, these are competently discussed and illustrated. Of great significance is the section dealing with athletic standards for various educational levels. Here, summaries of professional reports on the physiological, psychological, and sociological implications of participation and competition are admirably treated.

An ardent and intense student of athletics, Dr. Bucher is Professor of Education and Director of Graduate Study in Physical Education at New York University. His writings in the field of athletics and physical education are well known among professional colleagues. Ralph K. Dupee, Jr. has participated extensively in competitive athletics and presently is a coach of major sports at the Polytechnic Preparatory Country Day School in Brooklyn.

MOREY R. FIELDS
Content Editor

Contents

Athletics in
Schools and Colleges

CHAPTER I

The History of Athletics in Education

The athletics program in schools and colleges includes intramural, extramural, and varsity interscholastic and intercollegiate activities.

Definitions

Intramural athletics may be defined as "athletic competition in which all participants are students in the same school."[1] *Extramural athletics* involve "athletic competition in which participants are students from two or more schools,"[2] . . . [however,] "they differ from [varsity] interscholastics in that they seek to involve all students irrespective of skill; they usually involve only a day or two at the end of an intramural season: and they usually require few or no systematic practice sessions. . . . Extramural athletics "do not involve leagues, championships, or season-long schedules."[3] *Varsity interscholastic athletics* refers to competition among teams from different schools. "The school team . . . is usually composed of the most skilled players among all students [of one sex] in a school."[4] Varsity interscholastic athletics are characterized by teams playing season-long schedules in leagues, and by the determination of champions. A great amount of emphasis is placed on developing the team through intense, regularly scheduled practice sessions, and most of the games are played before spectators.[5] *Varsity intercollegiate athletics* have the same characteristics as interscholastic athletics, except that they are played at college and university levels.

The competitive athletics program is one phase of the total physical education program. The physical education program may be represented as a pyramid, in which the instructional classes or serv-

---

[1] Educational Policies Commission, *School Athletics* (Washington, D.C.: National Education Association, 1954), p. 23.
[2] *Ibid.*
[3] *Ibid.*
[4] *Ibid.*, p. 6.
[5] *Ibid.*

ice program are the base and the athletics program—an outgrowth
of the service program—is the peak.

This monograph will examine the role of competitive athletics in
the educational program, discuss the intramural, extramural, interscholastic and intercollegiate programs, identify problems associated
with the administration of these programs, and recommend administrative policies and standards at various educational levels.

History of Athletics in Education

In 1954, the Educational Policies Commission made the following statement about athletics:

> We believe in athletics as an important part of the school physical
> education program. We believe that the experience of playing ath-
> letic games should be a part of the education of all children and
> youth who attend school in the United States.
>
> Participation in sound athletic programs, we believe, contributes
> to health and happiness, physical skill and emotional maturity, social
> competence and moral values.
>
> We believe that cooperation and competition are both important
> components of American life. Athletic participation can help teach
> the values of cooperation as well as the spirit of competition.
>
> Playing hard and playing to win can help to build character. So
> also do learning to "take it" in the rough and tumble of vigorous
> play, experiencing defeat without whimpering and victory without
> gloating, and disciplining oneself to comply with the rules of the
> game and of good sportsmanship.
>
> Athletics may also exemplify the value of the democratic process
> and of fair play. Through team play, the student athlete often learns
> how to work with others for the achievement of group goals. Ath-
> letic competition can be a wholesome equalizer. Individuals on the
> playing field are judged for what they are and for what they can do,
> not on the basis of the social, ethnic, or economic group to which
> their families belong.
>
> We believe that school athletics are a potential educative force of
> great power that is not used so much as it should be and that is too
> often misused. We believe that concerted efforts should be made by
> school personnel and by other citizens to capitalize more effectively
> on the potential values in school athletics. . . .[6]

This statement represents a highly significant step in a long and
chaotic history of athletics in the schools of America. The athletics

---

[6] *Ibid.*, pp. 3–4.

program arose in response to student and community demand and its early years were marked by a lack of educational control. Only in the early twentieth century was the contribution of athletics to education formally recognized.

The history of athletics may be examined chronologically: the Colonial Period, the Post-Revolutionary Period; 1853 to 1885; 1886 to 1906; 1907 to 1930; and 1930 to the present.

Colonial Period. In Colonial America, the attitude toward sports and games was dictated by the conditions of life. The early colonists had very little opportunity to play. Any hope of survival was dependent on directing all available energy to the daily struggle to carve a settlement in the wilderness. The colonists were quick to recognize this basic fact by the adoption of strict regulations "in detestation of idleness."[7]

As the colonies grew, however, regional differences in attitudes toward play began to appear. In New England, the Calvinist tradition stressed all work and no play. This policy was based on the Puritan concept of evil as inherent in frivolous activity, which had developed in reaction to the customs of the upper middle classes of Europe. The early New England laws regarding play reflected this tradition.

Only on special occasions did the colonists of New England seek any enjoyment. On such holidays as Thanksgiving, hunts and contests of strength between the settlers and friendly Indians highlighted the festivities.[8] Militia training days were often marked by feasting and competition in target shooting, wrestling, running and jumping.[9] Even the children did not play in the early Colonial Period, but as times changed they were reported to enjoy such games as tag, marbles, leap frog, and kite flying.[10]

Outside New England, the colonists did not object to games and sports. Virginia originally enacted laws that were just as restrictive as those of New England because there was simply no time for play. As conditions improved, however, the more liberal Anglican outlook

----

[7] F. R. Dulles, *America Learns to Play* (New York: Appleton-Century-Crofts, Inc., 1940), p. 44.

[8] Robert B. Weaver, *Amusements and Sports in American Life* (Chicago: The University of Chicago Press, 1939), p.5.

[9] *Ibid.*

[10] *Ibid.*, p. 7.

that prevailed in the South gradually permitted the colonists there to take advantage of recreational opportunities. The colonists who had settled in this area were sports-loving enthusiasts who had brought to America many of the activities which had been popular in seventeenth-century England—cockfighting, horseracing, ninepins, hunting and fishing, marksmanship, and dice and card games.[11] Similarly, Dutch colonists in New Amsterdam participated in bowling, skating, coasting, sleighing, and various types of ball games.[12] Because most of the early colonists were Protestants, education in this period reflected the religious orientation characteristic of the contemporary Reformation Period in Europe. Education was conducted by religious groups to acquaint children with the religious duties and activities of the community. Colleges were designed primarily for the preparation of candidates for the ministry.[13] Consequently, sports or play activities were frowned upon and sternly disapproved by school faculties.[14]

Despite the opposition of the Puritans, amusements and athletics gained steadily in popularity from the beginning of the Colonial Period to the Revolutionary War. Only when the British exerted greater pressure on the colonies in the early 1770's were the New Englanders successful in exerting influence in the First Continental Congress to discourage such popular activities.[15]

Post-Revolutionary Period. The period following the Revolutionary War was marked by a rising interest in athletics. During the British occupation, the American colonists had come to appreciate the British love of amusements. By the latter part of the eighteenth century, many leading families in Boston and Philadelphia were enjoying "frivolous fun."[16] The early nineteenth century saw the rise of a few spectator sports. The contests were promoted by proprietors of resorts and railroads, and the participants were usually

---

[11] Dulles, *op. cit.*, p. 5.

[12] Parke Cummings, "History of Athletic Sports," *Encyclopedia Americana* (1957 ed.), 436.

[13] Harry A. Scott, *Competitive Sports in Schools and Colleges* (New York: Harper & Row, Publishers, 1951), p. 11.

[14] Seward Staley, "Next Step in School Sports," *Aims and Methods in School Athletics*, edited by E. Dana Coulkins (New York: Wingate Memorial Foundation, 1932), p. 32.

[15] Weaver, *op. cit.*, p. 17.

[16] *Ibid.*, p. 18.

professionals. Rowing and sailing regattas, wrestling and shooting matches, and foot races were the most popular activities.[17]

Concurrent with the development of athletics was the rise of the academy as an educational institution. The academies were private, nondenominational schools designed to prepare the student for life in the community. The more liberal and democratic philosophy of the academies emphasized the values of health, work, and play. Organized, school-sponsored recreational sports programs patterned after those in English schools were initiated. Probably the first school to integrate games and sports into the curriculum was Dummer Grammar School (Byfield, Massachusetts) in 1782.[18] Soccer and bat ball were played at Exeter early in the nineteenth century.[19]

Rowing was one of the first college sports. Yale adopted it in 1843; Harvard, in 1845. The first intercollegiate contest in America was the 1852 Harvard-Yale race for eight oared barges, which was won by Harvard.[20]

The period 1853–85. The years from 1853 to 1885 were characterized by rather slow growth in college athletics up to 1870 and a rather rapid growth from 1870 to 1885. This period was marked by the rising popularity of football and baseball, lawn tennis, handball, golf, rollerskating, ice hockey, and lacrosse. As these sports developed, students eventually organized competition on an intramural basis and on an extramural basis with nearby colleges. The contests were sponsored by the students against the wishes of hostile and unsympathetic faculties.[21]

The period 1886–1906. During the greater part of the period 1886–1906 the undergraduates managed the college sports program. The period is characterized by an expansion of the athletic program, which led eventually to a chaotic situation marked by short-range planning, emphasis on financially successful spectator sports, and extensive player recruiting. Training was intensified and coaches were hired. Equipment requirements grew in quantity and cost. All these innovations represented increasing expenditures,

[17] Cummings, *op. cit.,* p. 437.
[18] Scott, *op. cit.,* p. 12.
[19] Frederick D. Gruber and Thomas Bayard Beatty, *Secondary School Activities* (New York: McGraw-Hill Book Company, 1954), p. 8.
[20] Cummings, *loc. cit.*
[21] George E. Shepard and Richard D. Jamerson, *Interscholastic Athletics* (New York: McGraw-Hill Book Company, 1953), p. 3.

which called for additional funds. The students solicited support from the alumni, in return for which the alumni received a share in the control of athletics. Meanwhile, faculty members, although aware of the situation, maintained an indifferent attitude. Consequently, there was no struggle for control: the alumni won by default.[22]

Many of the abuses which are still evident in the school athletics program originated during this period. Skilled athletes were openly recruited by captains and team managers. Although there were few direct gifts of money, there were offers of nominal employment and promises of social favor and athletic success. Proselyting among educational institutions was also common during this period. Tramp athletes, or players who moved from organization to organization, were to be found on most teams. It was a common practice to make annual campaigns to draw players away from smaller colleges. It was easy to transfer from one college to another and registration of students in a single subject was a common practice.[23]

It was also during this period that colleges and universities recognized their common interests and began to form associations. The New England Association of Colleges and Preparatory Schools was founded in 1879; the College Association of Pennsylvania, in 1887; the Association of Colleges and Preparatory Schools of The Middle States and Maryland, in 1888; and The North Central Association of Colleges and Secondary Schools, in 1892. This movement was important in college athletics in affecting standards of eligibility for intercollegiate competition.[24]

The period 1907–30. The period 1907–30 was characterized by a more intense effort to organize and control athletics through greater faculty interest and through the formation of athletic associations. Greater faculty control grew out of a conviction that the college or university should be an institution of learning. The widening biosocial concept of education had given physical education a new meaning that included all bodily activity, both gymnastic and athletic. It was natural that faculties, charged with the responsibility

---

22 Howard J. Savage, *et al., American College Athletics,* Bulletin No. 23 (New York: The Carnegie Foundation for the Advancement of Teaching, 1929), p. 23.
23 *Ibid.,* p. 28.
24 *Ibid.,* p. 26.

of education, should now also take control of its physical aspects.[25] Athletic associations were established under faculty control, with some student and/or alumni representation. The athletic associations assumed responsibility for the entire athletic program.[26]

Meanwhile, numerous intercollegiate and athletic conferences and associations of school and colleges also began to assert themselves. The Intercollegiate Association of Amateur Athletes in America had been founded in 1875; the Intercollegiate Football Association, in 1876; the Western Conference ("Big Ten"), in 1895; and the Intercollegiate Athletic Association of the United States (later called the National Collegiate Athletic Association), in 1905.[27] By 1930, through the efforts of these newly formed associations and the work of the college faculties, the so-called principle of associative activity had been applied to athletics in a manner consistent with the contemporary educational philosophy.[28]

The place of athletics in education was further strengthened by the incorporation of athletics into the physical education curriculum. Up to this period, physical education had been devoted primarily to gymnastics designed to prevent or to correct physical deficiencies. Despite the considerable popularity of athletics in the community, sports and games were not included in the physical education program. The Boston Conference of 1889, believed by many to be one of the most important physical education conferences held in the United States, was indicative of the attitude of physical educators toward athletics: there was no prominent spokesman for sports and games, and athletic sports were mentioned only twice during the entire conference.[29] Cozens and Stumpf have attributed this so-called cultural lag to a number of factors. First, physical education teachers were unwilling to accept play as a part of the school program. Second, most of these teachers had basically a medical education as preparation for teaching gymnastics. Third, class size, class time, and existing facilities were not easily adapted to instruction in a sports program.[30]

---

25 *Ibid.*, p. 32.

26 Scott, *op. cit.*, p. 89.

27 Arthur Weston, *The Making of American Physical Education* (New York: Appleton-Century-Crofts, Inc., 1962), p. 43.

28 Savage *et al.*, *op. cit.*, p. 27.

29 Frederick W. Cozens and Florence S. Stumpf, *Sports in American Life* (Chicago: The University of Chicago Press, 1953), p. 63.

30 *Ibid.*, pp. 67–68.

Shortly before 1900, physical exercise and gymnastics had become requirements for a degree in many colleges and universities. The popularity of formal gymnastics rapidly decreased, to be replaced by a rise in intramural athletics. Started at the University of Michigan in 1913,[31] intramural athletics spread rapidly across the country. The competitive element inherent in athletics was largely responsible for the sudden popularity of intramurals.

At this same time, physical educators began to recognize the value of play in the educational program. They had become acquainted with Froebel's theory of play and the progressive movement of Kilpatrick, Hall, and Dewey, with its emphasis on the unity of the mind and body. Thomas D. Wood, Luther Gulick, and Clark Hetherington were the first to interpret the "new" physical education, which emphasized athletic skills in a manner consistent with general educational objectives. The transition to a program of play activity was given greater impetus by the poor physical fitness of draftees during World War I.

High school athletics had suffered seriously from the abuses which characterized the collegiate program at the turn of the century. It was only natural that the more spectacular and least beneficial aspects of college athletics were universally imitated by high school students. Regulation by various associations and, eventually, by the faculty was successful in correcting many of the abuses of the high school program. The New York Public School Athletic League was founded in 1903. State high school athletic associations, charged with developing uniform regulations, were formed in all the states by 1925. The National Federation of State High School Athletic Associations was formed in 1922.

The period 1930 to the present.   The period from 1930 to the present has been characterized by the increased desire of educational authorities to maintain control over the athletic program in order to insure the educational values inherent in participation in athletics. Much of the progress which has occurred has resulted from the efforts of various athletic leagues and conferences. The National Collegiate Athletic Association and the National Federation of State High School Athletic Associations are representative of recent trends.

---

[31] Savage *et al., op. cit.,* p. 30.

Historically, the National Collegiate Athletic Association (NCAA) was conceived as an educational organization with neither legislative nor executive functions. The NCAA developed as a result of the alarming number of football injuries which occurred at the turn of the century. In December 1905, Chancellor MacCracken of New York University called a conference to decide whether football should be abolished or reformed. It was decided to initiate reform. A second meeting was called, at which a football rules committee was appointed. This committee was united with the former American Football Rules Committee to establish a single rules committee. At this meeting, plans were also formulated for the organization of a national body, the Intercollegiate Athletic Association of the United States (IAA), to suggest sound practices for intercollegiate athletics. At a meeting in March 1906, a constitution and bylaws were adopted. At the fifth annual convention of the IAA (December 1910), the name was changed to the National Collegiate Athletic Association.

In the first constitution, a set of minimum eligibility rules were recommended, but were not conditions of membership. They restricted competition to full-time college students, limited competition to four years, required a year of residence for transfer students before eligibility, and provided a penalty of one year's eligibility for those football players not continuing in regular attendance at their college for two thirds of any year in which they played. In 1939, the constitution was revised: an explicit statement of standards was coupled with a demand for adherence to them and a provision for the expulsion of violators. After World War II, continued efforts to strengthen membership requirements culminated in the 1953 convention, at which the Council, a seventeen-man policy-making body, was vested with the authority to discipline members who failed to observe the rules and regulations of the association. Furthermore, the Council was authorized to direct members to avoid competition with other members who failed to observe the rules and regulations of the association.

Presently, the NCAA has both educational and legislative functions. Its basic objective is to promote uniform and high standards of athletic administration and competition. The NCAA formulates rules for intercollegiate sports; publishes rules and guidebooks; and conducts national championship meets or tournaments in cross-country, golf, tennis, basketball, baseball, boxing, gymnastics, wrestling, ice hockey, swimming, fencing, and track and field. In addition, the NCAA is a member of the United States Olympic Association. It is represented in committees for nine of the Olympic sports which are conducted as a part of the intercollegiate athletic program.

The National Federation of State High School Athletic Associations had a beginning similar to that of the NCAA. Already in existence at or shortly after the turn of the century were a number of state athletic associations. In 1920, L. W. Smith, secretary of the Illinois High School Athletic Association, invited representatives from the neighboring states of Indiana, Iowa, Michigan, and Wisconsin, to discuss problems resulting from high school contests organized by colleges, universities, clubs, and other promoters. In many cases eligibility rules and other regulations of high school groups had been ignored and chaos prevailed. At the meeting it was decided that a national organization was necessary in order to insure adequate control of high school athletics. A constitution and bylaws were adopted and the name—Midwest Federation of State High School Athletic Associations—was chosen. Four states—Wisconsin, Michigan, Illinois, and Indiana—formally ratified the constitution in 1921, thereby establishing themselves as charter members. The present name of the National Federation was chosen in 1922. Since then, the National Federation has grown to an organization that encompasses the state athletic associations of all states but Texas.

The National Federation is composed of legislative and executive bodies. The National Council, composed of one representative from each member state, is the legislative body. The Executive Committee is composed of one representative from each of the seven territorial sections defined in the constitution. In addition, a full-time executive staff coordinates and administers the program of the association.

The National Federation has made many contributions to high school athletics—the greatest, perhaps, was the set of eligibility requirements adopted in 1929, which included recommendations pertaining to age, semesters in schools, enrollment, scholarship, amateur status, independent team participation, transfer, recruiting, and awards. The National Federation has been the prime mover in eliminating "outlaw" teams from competition; in eliminating national championships; in requiring official sanction of interstate meets and tournaments; in establishing standards for the scheduling of interstate contests; in writing and/or adopting playing rules to meet the particular characteristics of the high school athlete; in making recommendations for price reduction and specifications in the manufacture of athletic equipment to be used at the high school level; in maintaining and approving interscholastic athletic records; in resolving national policies with regard to solicitation, national and sectional meets, and postseason and all-star contests; and in adopting a solicitation and contract agreement with professional baseball.

The work of these two organizations is representative of that of countless other athletic associations and conferences. Much of the progress manifest in the following trends, cited by Fred V. Hein, is the result of their combined efforts.

1. More discussion of the need and means of reinstating integrity and morality as high value attributes in our way of life.
2. An increasing unwillingness of school and college administrative officers and their boards to abdicate their responsibility for the control of athletic policies and practices.
3. The trend toward attaching greater value to scholarship which in time will tend to equate the prestige of academic achievement with that of athletics.
4. Legal affirmation of the right of boards of control to establish conditions of play and to determine eligibility of players.
5. The increasing willingness and capacity of athletic conferences and associations to discipline their recalcitrant members.
6. The formation of new conferences of schools and colleges dedicated to the belief that athletics are an integral part of education.
7. The tendency to broaden athletic programs to include more activities and more participants, serving to lessen the pressure on any one sport or activity.
8. An increasing willingness of college presidents and others in positions of authority to speak up and stand up for what is right and wholesome in sports.
9. The present fitness emphasis which, if utilized to its best advantage, can help to build a better appreciation of participation in sports and athletics.[32]

Despite the progress noted above, serious problems, resulting from an overemphasis on winning, remain. In many cases, the var-

---

[32] Fred V. Hein, "Athletics in American Education," *Professional Contributions No. 7* (Washington, D.C.: American Academy of Physical Education, 1961), pp. 19–20.

sity teams are overemphasized and other parts of the athletic program suffer. Varsity-type competition is introduced at the pre-high school level for the express purpose of developing better varsity teams. In some schools, double academic standards exist in order to keep athletes eligible.

Some coaches, under pressure to win, compromise their integrity, thereby risking injury to the players and sacrificing any opportunities to develop individual character. Dependence on gate receipts for the athletic program often leads to financial pressures which open the way for many of the abuses of athletics; e.g. playing night games to attract large crowds, playing games in bad weather rather than forego gate receipts, and accepting financial help from local benefactors.

To remove any trace of such practices, it is important that the lessons learned from the history of athletics be implemented.

1. School and college faculties and administrations must accept full responsibility and authority for the athletics program.

2. If the principle of regulation by association is to be effective, schools and colleges which are united into conferences and associations must adhere to the rules and regulations that have been set up. Likewise, the athletic conferences or associations must be firm, consistent, and objective in the penalties awarded to member schools which have violated, in action or spirit, the rules and regulation of the organization.

3. The public must be educated to the values inherent in athletics and to the malpractices which exist in order that they may withhold support from those practices which are undesirable.

Educational Values of Athletics

The educational values of athletics may be generally classified in one of three categories: physical fitness, individual development, and social development.

Physical fitness. Athletics contribute to physical fitness by developing organic vigor, neuromuscular skill, and desirable attitudes toward play and exercise. In order to develop and maintain a high degree of physical fitness, the individual must voluntarily submit to a vigorous program of exercise. Perhaps the strongest force capable of motivating the American boy to engage in strenuous conditioning programs is the desire to excel in competitive athletics. It is a well-known fact that "competitive athletic skills are among the chief sources of social esteem in the period preceding maturity."[33] Consequently, a boy will eagerly participate in vigorous conditioning programs to develop the strength, endurance, and skill necessary to excel in athletic competition, thereby enhancing his own peer status. The contribution to a high degree of physical fitness is an obvious concomitant.[34]

In order to achieve success in athletics, the individual must develop neuromuscular skills that will enable him to respond instantly and effectively to the numerous situations which arise during the game. The resulting skill development will enable the individual to accomplish the normal physical requirements of his work efficiently and to respond with ease to emergencies requiring unusual strength, endurance, speed, or coordination.[35]

The acquisition of skill through athletics leads to a high level of proficiency and the strong desire to engage in physical activity after graduation from school or college. William Solley, in a study of college freshman, concluded that students who had participated in interschool athletics in high school and elementary school devoted a greater proportion of their extraclass play time to intramural athletics and engaged in a significantly greater amount of physical activity during their freshman year.[36]

The potential value of athletics in creating a desire for further activity is important in maintaining physical fitness and preventing a variety of degenerative disease states which are caused by a lack of exercise.

Individual development. Self-realization, self-sufficiency, self-control, and self-discipline are individual qualities which can be developed through athletics. An individual's self-image is gained through comparing himself with others. In order to realize and assume his own role, the individual must be cognizant of the roles of

---

[33] H. E. Jones, "Physical Ability as a Factor in Social Adjustment in Adolescence," *Journal of Educational Research,* XL (December 1946), 29.

[34] Division of Men's Athletics of the American Association of Health, Physical Education, and Recreation, "Athletics in Education," *Journal of Health, Physical Education and Recreation,* XXXIII (September 1962), 24.

[35] *Ibid.*

[36] William H. Solley, "Relationship Between Participation in Interschool Sports and Extraclass Play Activities in College," *Research Quarterly,* XXXII (March 1961), 107.

others. Only by differentiating himself from others, and by perceiving *their* attitudes toward *him,* may the individual perceive his own self-image. Furthermore, his self-evaluation is based on a continuing perception of the attitudes of others toward himself. Therefore, an individual's conception of himself is dependent, in part, on having opportunities to observe others. The highly dynamic and competitive nature of athletics provides many such opportunities for comparison.

Self-sufficiency or self-reliance may be developed. Athletics provide an opportunity for the individual to make his own decisions and to profit from his mistakes, thereby gaining in ability for self-direction. One of the unfortunate outcomes of some contemporary coaching philosophies is that the players are not allowed to think for themselves; rather, they are directed from the sidelines. This practice may or may not win games, but it will most certainly deprive the participants of a highly valuable experience in decision-making.

Self-control may be developed. The ability to withstand or to adjust to emotional stress is believed to be a result of the stress adaptation mechanism which is conditioned by exercise. Mitchell, in reviewing the literature on stress adaptation, concluded that the increased adrenal activity which follows repetitive exercise increases the reserve of steroids which are available to counter stress. Likewise, lack of activity was reported to decrease the ability to withstand stress.[37]

Athletics not only provide the exercise leading to stress adaptation, they also present a highly charged atmosphere in which the individual may test and develop his ability to exercise self-control.

Self-discipline may also be developed. Participation and success in athletics requires a great deal of self-sacrifice. The individual is called upon to subordinate his own wishes and desires to those of the group; he is called upon to accept the consequences of his decisions, right or wrong; and he is expected to submit to strenuous conditioning programs and rigid training rules. The sacrifices which are required lead to the development of both mental and physical discipline.

Social development. Competition and cooperation are provided

---

[37] Ernest D. Mitchell, Jr., "Stress Adaptation Through Exercise," *Research Quarterly,* XXVIII (March 1957), 53.

through athletics. May and Doob state: "It is generally agreed that
the Western European and North American cultures (with the exception of certain minority groups) are basically more competitive
than cooperative."[38] Ours is a society that accepts competition as
desirable. Competition is a part of our way of life—a part to which
we attribute a great deal of our progress and high standard of living.
At the same time, America is a democratic nation which demands
cooperation, self-sacrifice, and respect for others. Competition and
cooperation must, therefore, be interdependent.

It is the proper function of the school, in transmitting the cultural heritage of the society, to provide opportunities for the individual to develop his capacity for cooperation and competition.
Jersild has stated:

> During the elementary school years, the child gains in his capac-
> ity for cooperation and teamwork. In order to realize his potential-
> ities, he must have a chance to practice. Cooperation involves the
> learning of certain techniques and skills; and these can best be
> learned in group situations.[39]

Jersild goes on to say:

> . . . the school must provide opportunities not only for coopera-
> tion, but also for wholesome forms of competition. In the past,
> there perhaps has been too much emphasis on competition. On the
> other hand, if schools tried to rout out all conditions which might
> involve children in competition, the youngsters themselves would
> find ways to compete.[40]

Athletics provide a natural opportunity to achieve this dual objective, for they are "competitive by nature and cooperative by ne-
cessity."[41] An individual must first compete with other members of
the team for a position; then he must cooperate with his teammates
as they compete with another team.

Sportsmanship may also be developed. Sportsmanship is a social
quality which implies fairness, adherence to the rules, understanding
and respect for individual differences, and the ability to accept de-
feat graciously. These qualities may be applied equally well to the

---

[38] M. A. May and L. W. Doob, "Competition and Cooperation" *Bulletin of
Social Sciences Research Council*, XXV (1937), 81.

[39] Arthur T. Jersild *et al., Child Development and the Curriculum* (New York:
Teachers College, Bureau of Publications, Columbia University, 1946), p. 131.

[40] *Ibid.*, p. 25.

[41] Educational Policies Commission, *op. cit.*, p. 16.

play situation or to life in a society which sets up certain moral and ethical codes. Sportsmanship may be developed in a properly controlled play situation with uncompromised leadership.

Objectives of Athletics

The objectives of an athletics program, therefore, include the following:

1. To develop and maintain the organic system;
2. To develop useful neuromuscular skills;
3. To develop individual self-reliance;
4. To develop socially desirable standards of conduct in a democratic society;
5. To develop an appreciation of the values of participation in athletics.

CHAPTER II

The Intramural Athletics Program

The major objective of the intramural program is to provide an opportunity for all students to benefit from the values of competition, irrespective of their skill. The slogan, "Athletics for All," accurately describes the role of intramurals in educational institutions.

Values

The following are some of the values that may be achieved through an intramural program of participation:

1. The improved physical well-being of the individual through participation in healthful activity.

2. The development of skills which may lead to a more lasting interest in athletic activities.

3. Fun and enjoyment.

The University of Washington's *Intramural Sports Handbook* lists the following objectives:

1. To promote health;
2. To increase physical fitness and physical skill;
3. To aid in social adjustment, personality and character development;
4. To encourage the desirable use of leisure time.[1]

The University of Connecticut Men's *Intramural Sports Handbook* lists these objectives:

1. To provide for students opportunities for fun, enjoyment, and fellowship through sports participation;

2. To give students opportunities to improve their health and physical fitness status through participation in vigorous sports;

3. To provide students with opportunities to release tensions and feelings of aggression in socially acceptable manners; and to receive ego satisfaction and a feeling of achievement through sports participation in order to maintain mental or emotional health.[2]

---

[1] University of Washington, *Intramural Sports Handbook, 1963–1964* (Seattle: University of Washington), p. 31.

[2] School of Physical Education, The University of Connecticut, *Men's Intramural Sports Handbook, 1963–1964* (Storrs, Conn.: University of Connecticut), p. 5.

Organization and Administration
of Intramural Athletics

Types of organization. The intramural program should provide students with the greatest possible amount of participation in the administration of the program while maintaining continuity in the program. Ideally, a plan giving the students full control over the program is advantageous from the standpoint of developing the capacity for democratic self-government. Such a plan, however, has serious limitations. First, students are in school only for a certain number of years. Thus any student administration would be constantly changing, leading to confusion and lack of continuity. Second, students are not trained in the techniques of effective administration. The result is that student management tends to be characterized either by too few students doing all the work or by too many students with constantly shifting responsibilities.

Therefore, a more effective plan is one in which one faculty member is designated as the director of intramural athletics and is assisted by a student intramural council. Under the guidance of such a director (one trained in the administration and organization of intramural athletics), the intramural council would determine all the policies and activities of the intramural program. Such a plan would provide continuity in the intramural program while permitting students to share in the making of policy. It has the added advantage of allowing the intramural director to settle disputes and protests; students often find it is difficult to do so without incurring hard feelings.

One very popular type of organization may be called the "pyramid" pattern. This plan, operated by students under the direction of a faculty member, takes many forms. At Princeton University, the Intramural Athletic Association is composed of a faculty director, a senior board, a junior board, and a sophomore board. The senior board—consisting of seven to nine men elected to the position of president, vice president, secretary, treasurer, publicity director, and alternates, respectively—is selected from the twelve- to sixteen-man junior board. The junior board has the responsibility of supervising the progress of the various leagues and tournaments. The members of this board are chosen from the group of sophomore dormitory managers who govern the activities of their respective dormitory teams. Managers are promoted by the senior board and the faculty director each year. Each manager eligible to move into a higher position is rated on the following points: attendance, performance of duties, efficiency, initiative, and knowledge of the program. The junior and senior boards meet with the faculty director to coordinate activities, discuss rules and regulations, and propose future plans. In effect, they function as an intramural council or board.[3]

This system is advantageous: the program is student-centered, yet continuity is maintained through a process of promotion through the ranks. The number of individuals needed at each level of the "pyramid" naturally varies with the size and scope of the particular intramural program.

The organization and administration of intramural athletics at Miami University (Oxford, Ohio) is directed by a student executive committee. The committee is composed of a student director and six student representatives—two from each of three intramural divisions. The purpose of the student committee is to organize and conduct the intramural program, to hear protests, and to make any rules changes it deems necessary. The actions of the committee are subject to approval by a faculty advisory committee composed of the intramural coordinator, two members of the physical and health education department, one freshman adviser, and a student representative. A student publicity director, elected by the executive committee, is responsible for all publicity pertaining to the intramural program. Each residence hall or fraternity elects an athletic chairman who becomes responsible for the entry of teams and individuals in each sport in the program. A team manager is, in turn, responsible for the organization and administration of each team within the residence hall or fraternity.[4]

Such a system can be easily adapted to the high school situation. Student representatives elected from each class and the intramural director could act as an advisory committee when necessary. The advantage of this plan is that the success of the intramural administration is not dependent on the student's going through a four-year "pyramid." Therefore, this system is able to tolerate a more tran-

[3] Department of Physical Education and Athletics, Princeton University, *Handbook of Intramural Sports, 1963–1964* (Princeton, N.J.: Princeton University), pp. 11–12.
[4] Department of Physical and Health Education for Men, Miami University, *Intramural Athletics* (Oxford, Ohio: Miami University), pp. 6–7.

sient student population, such as is likely to be found in the public school.

Units of competition. The selection of units of competition varies according to the level of education. In general, however, units should be chosen in a manner that will insure equal competition and afford the greatest opportunity for participation by all students.

In the elementary schools and junior and senior high schools, physical education classes, interclass rivalry, and homeroom competition are the most popular choices. The physical education class is a good unit because teams can easily be organized and captains and officials selected. It is important, however, that regular class time not be devoted to intramural competition. Competition between Freshman, Sophomore, Junior, and Senior classes may be effective in a small school, but the tendency of such a system is to limit severely the number of participants in the intramural program if only four teams are used. It might be more desirable to use this system as a supplement to another plan of organization. Classification of students by homeroom is quite common in many schools today and provides a natural unit for the stimulation of rivalry and competition.

In colleges and universities, numerous methods of selection are used and, in most cases, several different types are employed. Interclass competition is a popular climax to intramural competition when a premium is placed on outstanding ability. Sororities and fraternities are obvious units of competition in those colleges and universities which permit the existence of such organizations. The danger is that the independent students, many of whom would greatly benefit from competition, are neglected. Numerous plans designed to include the independents in intramurals have been proposed. One of the most popular is the ward or zone plan, according to which the community in which the students live is divided into a number of zones. (Postal zones or election wards are convenient units.) Competition would then proceed on an interzone basis. In colleges that have no sororities or fraternities, dormitory units are ideal. Some universities are organized into colleges or departments, and competition on an intercollege or interdepartmental level is very satisfactory. In some cases, equal competition and equal opportunity to participate may be assured by combining several units into one larger unit or by providing additional leagues for *B* or *C* teams.

At the University of Kentucky,[5] competition among men students is conducted at the fraternity, dormitory, and independent levels. At Florida State University,[6] teams are selected from fraternities, dormitories, and off-campus living units. In Brazosport School District (Texas),[7] competition is conducted on a homeroom basis.

Points and awards. Various types of award systems based on points have been devised as an incentive to participation in intramural athletics. Some systems are based on individual participation, with a cumulative point total necessary to receive a letter or some similar award. Other systems are based on group participation, with the award going to the group having the highest number of points. Some schools combine both types.

Arguments in favor of the award system are based on the premise that recognition is a necessary incentive or stimulus for participation in the intramural program. Arguments against the system maintain that awards represent an unnecessary, artificial incentive, a needless expense, and a possible form of discrimination against less skilled individuals.

Ideally, awards are not essential to intramural programs. A public relations program which stresses the recreational and social values of athletics will encourage participation for the values inherent in the activities rather than for awards or other material objects of recognition. Awards based on point systems are often unsatisfactory because they emphasize winning and tend to favor team sports, which are most easily adapted to a point system. The result is that students tend to select those sports in which they can get the most points rather than those which they would enjoy or which would yield the greatest carryover value. A point system also requires unnecessary bookkeeping. Nevertheless, award systems based on points exist in most college and high school intramural programs.

---

[5] University of Kentucky, *Intramural Sports for Men and Women, 1963–1964* (Lexington, Ky.: University of Kentucky), p. 33.

[6] Florida State University, *Intramural Handbook for 1963–64* (Tallahassee, Fla.: Florida State University), p. 12.

[7] H. E. Hooper, Director, Athletics and Physical Education, Brazosport Independent School District, Brazosport, Texas, in a letter (March 1964) to the authors.

The following principles, consistent with the objectives stated earlier, will insure a proper perspective to the point system:

1. The point system should reward participation, rather than ability. Thus, a group which uses many players should earn more points than one using only a few good players.

2. The point system should be simple and require a minimum of bookkeeping. Point penalties for defaults, unpunctuality, and the like, should be avoided.

3. If more points are awarded to team sports than to individual sports, it should be because more students participate in them and not because team sports carry a greater importance.

The scoring system of the Amarillo Public Schools (Texas) is typical of those used in most high schools.[8] Twenty-five points are awarded for first place in each sport; fifteen points, for second; ten points, for third; and five points, for fourth. Five additional points are awarded for each game played and five points for each player participating in each game. Competition is organized on a homeroom basis, and the team that accumulates the greatest number of points during a school year receives the school intramural trophy (which it keeps until the next year) enscribed with homeroom number, year, and teacher's name.

The following point system, used at Stanford University, is based on the classification of sports according to the nature of the game. Each year a permanent trophy is awarded to the unit accumulating the highest number of points for that year. Note that the classifications are based on the number of participants.

GROUP I

This group includes touch football, basketball, bowling, softball, and volleyball, in which entering teams are assigned to leagues composed of several teams each for a season of round-robin play. Upon the completion of league play, the several league leaders compete in an elimination tournament for the University championship in that sport. Points are awarded for Group 1 sports as follows:

University champions 70
Runners-up 40

Units entering two teams in any sport shall be placed in "A" and "B" divisions accordingly. League points shall be awarded as follows:

---

[8] S. Gergeni, Director, Health, Physical Education, and Safety, Amarillo Independent School District, Amarillo, Texas, in a letter (March 1964) to the authors.

	A	B
League winners	30	15
Second	20	10
Third	10	5
Fourth	5	3

Teams competing in the play-off tournament of any sport failing to reach the final round shall receive two intramural points for each game won. First-round byes will not count as games won.

A team which forfeits by nonappearance any matched game will lose all points in that sport unless provision has been made for the nonappearance.

GROUP II

Group II consists of horseshoes, tennis, table tennis, and any others whereby the entering teams are drawn into a bracket-form elimination tournament. Points are awarded in this group as follows:

Teams losing their first round of play shall receive 2 intramural points. Winners of their first round of play shall receive 4 points, and for each successive win to the semifinals a team shall accumulate 2 additional points. Teams losing in semifinal play shall receive a total of 12 points; the final loser, 16; and the tournament winner, 25.

No points will be awarded any team that forfeits a round of competition by nonappearance, regardless of what matches already have been played.

GROUP III

Group III consists of such sports as track, cross-country, gymnastics, and swimming, where all the teams are pitted against each other in one meet and scoring is awarded to place winners as follows (place points for all events are 5–4–3–2–1):

Meet winners	25
Second	16
Third	13
Fourth	10
Fifth	8
Sixth	6
Other finalists	2

GROUP IV

Group IV consists of dual activities such as wrestling, where winners are determined from each of several classifications within the sport. Place points shall be determined as follows:

Six or more competing:	Winner	6
	Finals	4
	Semifinals	2
	Others competing	1

Less than six competing: Winner 4

Finals 2

Others competing 1

Intramural points for the first six places shall be awarded as under Group III; all others competing, 2 points each.[9]

Some schools also make individual awards on the basis of points accumulated. At the University of Kentucky,[10] an all-year trophy is awarded to the individual with the highest number of points in intramural competition according to the following point schedule:

Winner in any sport: 5 points
Runner-up in any sport: 3 points
Third place in any sport: 1 point
Each contest won until the finals: 1 point
Each match or contest participated in: 1 point

Most girls' or women's athletics associations use some type of point system for making awards to individuals. With few exceptions, intramural and extramural programs are the summit of the competitive athletics program for women. In most schools the Women's Athletic Association (WAA) assumes responsibility for these programs and sets up an award system based on participation and contributions to WAA. At the University of Kentucky, points are awarded for several types of participation in WAA. For instance, a point is given for participation in any tournament, provided the individual plays in all scheduled games. In addition, a maximum of five points may be earned each year in the following ways:[11]

Participating in three fourths of a team's practice: 1 point
Working on a committee: 1 point
Participating on a team: 1 point
Membership on the Athletic Council of the WAA: 1 point
Serving as a team manager: 1 point
Officiating at team games: 1 point

A letter is awarded when a girl has accumulated fifteen points. It is interesting to note that a town girl who is not affiliated with an organization for which she may participate is awarded a letter for

---

[9] Stanford University, *Intramural Handbook, 1963–1964* (Stanford, Calif.: Stanford University), p. 9–10.

[10] University of Kentucky, *op. cit.*, p. 35, 37.

[11] *Ibid.*, p. 15.

an accumulation of ten points. A second award of a gold bowl is given for thirty points. A silver bowl is awarded for forty-five points, and a special gift is given to any girl accumulating sixty points.

The University of Connecticut *Men's Intramural Sports Handbook* places the question of awards in proper perspective:

> We hope that you will engage in the intramural program not primarily to win an award, but principally because you enjoy participating in sports activities. We hope further that you will recognize that the award has little value in itself, and that its principal value is that it represents the striving for excellence.[12]

Activities. The selection of a program of activities must be influenced by the size of the school, its location, the age group to be served, and the facilities that are available. The activities listed below may be used in an intramural program. Such a list is not all-inclusive. The success of any program depends on the ability of its director to improvise and adapt activities to his particular situation.

Suggested Intramural Activities

Archery	Fencing	Rowing
Badminton	Field hockey	Sailing
Baseball	Figureskating	Shuffleboard
Basketball	Flag football	Skiing
Bicycling	Football	Skish
Billiards	Free throws	Soccer
Bowling	Golf	Softball
Bridge	Gymnastics	Speedball
Canoeing	Handball	Squash
Checkers	Horseshoes	Swimming
Chess	Ice hockey	Table tennis
Crew	Kickball	Tennis
Cricket	Lacrosse	Touch football
Croquet	Newcomb	Track
Cross-country	Paddle tennis	Twenty-one
Darts	Polo	Volleyball
Deck tennis	Rifle shooting	Water polo
Dodge ball	Rollerskating	Wrestling

At the University of Chicago, the men's intramural program includes the following activities:[13]

---

[12] University of Connecticut, *op. cit.,* p. 14.
[13] The University of Chicago, *Intercollegiate and Intramural Athletics for Men, 1963–1964* (Chicago: The University of Chicago), p. 31.

Fall	*Winter*	*Spring*
Cross-country	Badminton	Bowling
Football	Basketball	Golf
Golf	Free throws	Horseshoes
Swimming	Handball	Softball
Tennis	Rifle shooting	Table tennis
Wrestling	Table tennis	Tennis
	Track	Volleyball

The University of Oregon's men's intramural program includes the following activities:[14]

Basketball	Swimming
Bowling	Tennis
Golf	Touch football
Handball	Track
Softball	Volleyball
	Wrestling

The Women's Athletic Association of the University of Kentucky sponsors competition in archery, badminton, basketball, bowling, golf, softball, swimming, table tennis, tennis, and volleyball. In addition, it sponsors extramural teams in basketball, hockey, softball, and tennis.[15]

The Moses Lake High School (Moses Lake, Washington) offers the following activities:[16]

Men	*Women*	*Coeducational*
Badminton	Badminton	Badminton
Flag football	Hit pin baseball	Volleyball
Gymnastics	Ping-pong	
Softball	Soccer	
Table tennis	Softball	
Track	Track	
Tumbling	Tumbling	
Volleyball	Volleyball	
Wrestling		

The Brazosport School District (Texas) includes scholastic events in its program of intramural activities. These schools sponsor com-

---

14 School of Health, Physical Education and Recreation, University of Oregon, *Handbook of Intramural Sports, 1963–1964* (Eugene, Ore.: University of Oregon), p. 13.

15 University of Kentucky, *op. cit.,* p. 11–14.

16 J. Adamson, Director, Physical Education and Athletics, Moses Lake School District, Moses Lake, Washington, in a letter (March 1964) to the authors.

petition in speech, mathematics, music, literary activities, spelling, cake baking, and dressmaking, as well as athletics. These events yield points according to the same system used for athletic events.[17]

Organization for Competition

In organizing teams for competition, some type of tournament system is usually followed. Several popular types of tournaments are used in scheduling intramural contests. These same tournaments are often used to make up league schedules. They include round-robin, single-elimination, double-elimination, and ladder tournaments.

Round-robin tournament. The round-robin tournament is most often used in scheduling seasonal sports, such as touch football, basketball, or softball. The round-robin system is effective because it allows a maximum amount of competition. If more than eight teams are competing, however, it would be advantageous to have two smaller leagues with a championship play-off tournament at the end of the regularly scheduled play. In this type of tournament, each team in the league plays every other team. Thus, if there are eight teams in a league, each team would play a seven-game schedule. The total number of contests played in a round-robin tournament is equal to one half the product of the number of teams times the number of teams minus 1, or $\frac{N(N-1)}{2}$. If there are eight teams in the league, there will be $\frac{8(8-1)}{2}$, or twenty-eight contests.

The schedule may be arranged in one of several possible methods. Probably the easiest is the vertical-rotation method. Each of an even number of teams is assigned a number. The numbers are arranged in two columns, in the manner indicated below. Then, with the 1 kept in a fixed position, the other numbers are rotated in a clockwise direction, one position at a time, until each reaches its initial position. For example:

1	5		1	2		1	3		1	4
2	6		3	5		4	2		8	3
3	7		4	6		8	5		7	2
4	8		8	7		7	6		6	5

---

[17] H. E. Hooper, *op. cit.*

Table 1 illustrates the rotation for an eight-team league. The Roman numerals indicate the playing date.

TABLE 1
ROUND-ROBIN ROTATION

I. 1 vs. 5	II. 1 vs. 2	III. 1 vs. 3
2 vs. 6	3 vs. 5	4 vs. 2
3 vs. 7	4 vs. 6	8 vs. 5
4 vs. 8	8 vs. 7	7 vs. 6
IV. 1 vs. 4	V. 1 vs. 8	VI. 1 vs. 7
8 vs. 3	7 vs. 4	6 vs. 8
7 vs. 2	6 vs. 3	5 vs. 4
6 vs. 5	5 vs. 2	2 vs. 3
VII. 1 vs. 6		
5 vs. 7		
2 vs. 8		
3 vs. 4		

If the number of teams in the league is uneven, one team draws a bye for each playing date. For vertical-rotation scheduling, the bye is kept constant and all other numbers are rotated in a clockwise direction. For a five-team league, the pairings are as shown in Table 2.

TABLE 2
ROUND-ROBIN ROTATION

I. 1 vs. 4	II. 2 vs. 1	III. 3 vs. 2
2 vs. 5	3 vs. 4	5 vs. 1
3 bye	5 bye	4 bye
IV. 5 vs. 3	V. 4 vs. 5	
4 vs. 2	1 vs. 3	
1 bye	2 bye	

Another method for round-robin pairings is the graphical box method shown in Table 3.

TABLE 3
ROUND-ROBIN GRAPHICAL PAIRING

Team	A	B	C	D	E
A		1	2	3	4
B			3	4	5
C				5	1
D					2
E					

In the first horizontal row, starting in the second column, consecutive numbers are placed under each team from left to right. In the second horizontal row, numbering begins in the third column, with the next higher number than is above it in the first horizontal row. If at any time the number corresponding to the number of teams in the league is used, the next consecutive number is 1. In the example above, there are five teams in the league. In the third horizontal row the number 5 appears, followed immediately by 1. Each of the numbers within the graph indicates the round or playing date. For instance, in the first round, *A* would play *B*, and *C* would play *E*. In the fifth round, *B* would play *E*, and *C* would play *D*.

If time permits, and there are not too many teams competing, a double round-robin may be held. To make the second set of pairings, simply repeat the vertical rotation or graphical methods.

Single-elimination tournament. The single-elimination tournament is well suited to individual or dual sports, in which there is little time to complete the tournament and determine a champion.

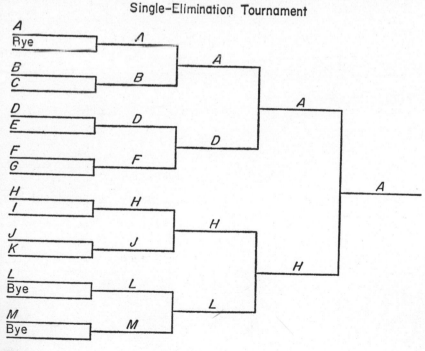

Single–Elimination Tournament

Fig. 1

Tennis, golf, badminton, wrestling, and squash are well suited for this type of tournament. Often, a single-elimination tournament is used to decide the champion from among several league winners in round-robin tournaments. In the single-elimination tournament, a number of lines equal to some power of 2 (2, 4, 8, 16, 32, 64, and so on) is used. If the number of entries does not equal a given power of 2, the next highest power of 2 must be employed. For instance, if there are thirteen entries, there will be sixteen lines. It will therefore be necessary to have three byes; those players drawing them will proceed to the next round of play without opposition. Figure 1 is an example of a sixteen-line single-elimination tournament with thirteen entries and three byes.

If the number of byes in the single-elimination tournament is even, place an equal number in the upper and lower halves of the brackets. If the number is uneven, place the extra bye in the lower bracket.

Single-Elimination Tournament with Seedings

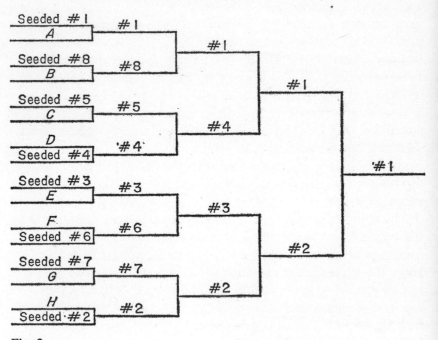

Fig. 2

When possible, it is best to seed the single elimination. Seeding prevents two good players from meeting in an early round of the tournament and one being eliminated by the other. If seeded players are placed in different brackets in the lower and upper halves, the better players will not meet until the quarter- or semifinal rounds.

Normally, the better players are rated and seeded according to the following pattern. The remaining positions are assigned by drawing the names of the other entrants. A bracket with eight seeded players is shown in Fig. 2. If there are not enough players for a full bracket and byes must be assigned, they are often given to the seeded players in order of rank or by drawing.

Double-elmination tournament. A double-elimination tournament may be used if time permits. In this type of tournament, a team must lose twice before being eliminated. The advantage of this organization is that an individual or team may have a bad day and still win the tournament. This system is used only when there are eight or fewer teams or individuals. The organization of a double-elimination tournament is shown in Fig. 3. The losers of the first round are placed in a separate bracket. The winner of the losers' tournament—in this case, Team 2—plays the winner of the winners' bracket for the championship. If the champion of the winners' bracket, Team 1, beats Team 2, then Team 1 is champion, because Team 2 had already lost its first game; however, Team 2 must beat Team 1 twice in order to win the final play-offs, because Team 1 has not lost any games.

Ladder tournament. A ladder tournament is particularly well-suited for individual and dual sports, such as handball or tennis. The participants are listed in a vertical "ladder" that permits the transfer of names during the tournament. The object is to get to the top rung of the ladder by challenging those teams that occupy higher rungs. It is important that the rules for challenging be clearly understood by all participants. Normally, a contestant may challenge the one above him. If the lower-placed contestant wins, the two exchange positions on the ladder. The loser is not allowed to challenge the contestant above until he defeats the man below. A contestant can move up the ladder in this manner until he reaches the top. If a challenge is accepted by the contestant above at the same time that another challenge is received from below, the two contestants occupying the highest positions on the ladder play their

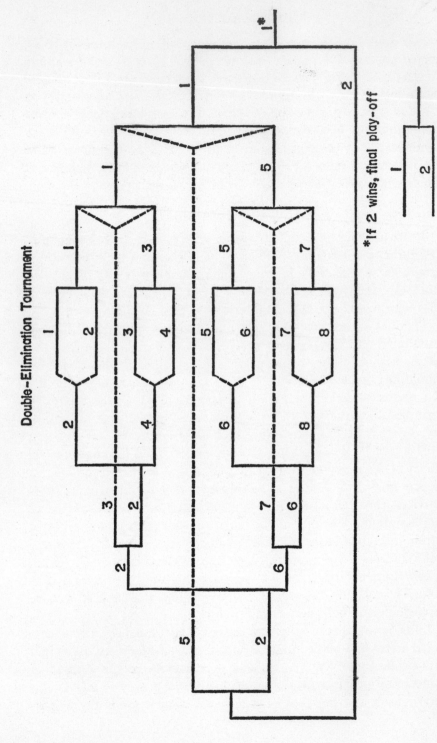

Double-Elimination Tournament

*If 2 wins, final play-off

Fig. 3

match first. All challenges must be accepted, unless previously accepted challenges have not been played. In order to avoid stalling, a time limit, within which a challenge must be played off, should be established. Often, the top four or five entries will participate in a round-robin or single- or double-elimination tournament for the championship. The advantage of a ladder tournament is that it is administered by the participants, who merely report their scores to the intramural office. The participants schedule their matches at their own convenience and act as their own officials.

Eligibility in Intramurals

There are four points of concern in the general area of eligibility for intramural athletics: scholastic eligibility, professional status, varsity letter winners, and group membership. It is well to keep in mind that the general objective is participation for all. The policies with respect to eligibility must reflect this basic philosophy.

There is almost general agreement that there should be no scholastic eligibility requirements for participation in intramurals. The feeling is that so long as an individual is enrolled in the school, he should be eligible to participate in its intramural athletics program. The provision that scholastically deficient individuals should not be permitted to participate in intramurals is difficult to support or justify. There is little evidence that such action increases the student's attention to his studies; quite the opposite is often the case: the removal of the enjoyment of participation and the opportunities for success may actually divert the student's attention to less desirable activities. The intramural program has often been characterized as the "laboratory section" of the physical education course. It is in intramural athletics that the individual is able to apply the skills and techniques he has mastered in his classes. The intramural program is, therefore, a very important experience in the child's total education. As such, the opportunity to participate in it should not be dependent on scholastic record.

In an intramural program emphasizing participation, the professional status of a player must be considered. Certainly an individual with professional status in a given sport should not be allowed to compete at an intramural level in that sport; however, there is no good reason why he should not have an equal opportunity to participate in other sports. Some would go so far as to allow a professional player to play in that sport if a year has elapsed after his last professional performance. Although such a practice may not be entirely feasible, it is based on the principle of providing maximum participation for all students.

The question of letter winners and varsity squad members arises often. It is generally agreed that an individual who has won a varsity award in a sport should be ineligible for the intramural program in that sport only. This provision is interpreted to mean that a letterman in football cannot play touch football, and a letterman in baseball cannot play softball. Likewise, a member of a varsity team in a sport is normally ineligible to participate in that sport during the season. In some systems, a varsity athlete is not eligible to participate in any intramural sports during the season.

The following eligibility regulations of the men's intramural program at the University of Washington are typical of those in effect throughout the nation:

Section A. Men who have won their varsity letter, including junior varsity crew award, are not eligible for intramural competition in their letter sport. This provision also applies to transfer letter winners from colleges or universities granting a bachelor's degree. Letter winners are also ineligible for comparable intramural sports as follows: football for flag football, baseball for softball.

Section B. Freshmen numeral winners and junior college transfer letter winners are ineligible for intramural competition in the sport in which they won their awards, until they have had a chance to establish themselves as members of varsity squads. When dropped from the varsity squad because of lack of ability, these award winners will become immediately eligible for the sport in question. Freshman numeral winners and junior college transfer letter winners who do not turn out for the varsity become eligible for intramural competition after one varsity season has elapsed.

Section C. Men who are members of varsity, freshman, or other teams competing on an intercollegiate basis, after final team selection has been made or after conference competition has begun, are not eligible for any intramural participation during the quarter in which the intercollegiate sport is active.

Section D. Men who are candidates for the varsity, freshman, or other teams competing on an intercollegiate basis are not eligible for any intramural competition during the quarter in which they are preparing for a sport that is to become active in the succeeding quarter, except by written permission of the head coach.

Section E. An athlete shall be ineligible to participate in the sport in which he has become professionalized.

Section F. Persons who have won two championships in singles competition are ineligible for further singles play in the sport. Persons who have won an individual event twice are ineligible for further participation in the event. Members of a championship doubles team are ineligible to compete further as a team.

Section G. A player having entered a contest with a team may not transfer to another team in the sport except with the approval of the Intramural Board.

Section H. A player must have participated in league play to be eligible for championship play-offs. In single-elimination tournaments, championship play-offs will be considered to be the semi-final and final rounds. A team winning a game by forfeit shall be allowed to consider all players appearing for the contest and listed on the scoresheet as having participated.[18]

Financing Intramurals

As part of the total physical education program, the intramural program should share in an equitable manner in the budget allotted to the physical education department. Ideally, the physical education budget, which includes funds for service classes, intramurals, extramurals, and interscholastics or intercollegiates, should come from the general education budget of the school. Unfortunately, many schools and colleges have found that the intramural program must be self-sufficient and produce its own operating income if it is to continue. Many sources of income are used. In some cases, a fixed percentage of the gate receipts is applied to intramurals. The major disadvantage to this plan is that gate receipts vary greatly from year to year, and it is therefore difficult for an intramural director to know how much money to anticipate. In many colleges and universities, the students are annually assessed an activity fee which is divided among the various extracurricular activities on campus. The intramural programs for men and women are normally included within the activity-fee schedule. This plan proves satisfactory for colleges and universities, but students in the public schools can hardly be expected to pay a student activity fee. In some programs, entry fees are charged and fines for defaults and postponements are assessed. Such a plan really defeats the objectives of participation

---

[18] University of Washington, *op. cit.*, p. 33, 34.

and is difficult to justify from an educational standpoint. A nominal admission is charged in some quarters, which helps to defray part of the cost of the program. In many cases, money-making concessions or carnivals are sponsored by the intramural councils. Numerous other fund-raising techniques have been used.

The principle to be applied in the financing of intramurals is that they are an integral part of the educational process and should, therefore, have a proportionate share in the educational budget of the school.

Scheduling Intramurals

The physical education program may be conceived as a pyramid: the base is the service program; the middle sections, the intramural and extramural programs; and the apex, the interscholastic or intercollegiate athletics program. Priorities for equipment, personnel, and facilities should follow the same order. Unfortunately, there is, in practice, a tendency for the service program and the athletics program to "squeeze out" the intramural and extramural programs and leave them to fend for themselves. This is not educationally sound. The priorities recommended above reflect the number of students benefiting from each phase of the physical education program. Because the intramural and extramural programs benefit more individuals than does the varsity program, it follows logically that they should get priority over the latter. Only after good intramural and extramural programs are established and functioning should the interscholastic and intercollegiate program be instituted. Athletics are as important for the physically gifted child as advanced placement or enrichment courses are for the academically gifted child. Just as elementary mathematics and science courses, with their laboratories, precede advanced courses in these fields, so must service classes, with their laboratories (intramurals and extramurals) precede the varsity athletics program. Therefore, any consideration regarding personnel and facilities should be given first to the intramural and extramural programs and secondly to the interscholastic and intercollegiate programs.

In colleges and universities, the difficulty of scheduling time for intramural and extramural activities is somewhat alleviated because most of the students live on or near the campus and can participate all afternoon and part of the evening. This is not true in the public schools, where students live some distance from the school and often must rely on school buses for transportation. The problem is magnified by the fact that many students may have after-school jobs or other responsibilities. Several alternatives have been proposed. One is that intramural and extramural programs be conducted immediately after school and before varsity athletic practice begins. This is probably the best time for most schools. In schools with a large bus-transported population, the last period of the day is often set aside for activities, including intramurals and extramurals. Some schools schedule intramurals during the lunch hour. This practice is somewhat controversial: it cannot be condoned for swimming and the more strenuous sports; for more passive, recreational-type activities—such as horseshoes, table tennis, and softball—it is well-suited. The danger in a lunch-hour program is that participants will either eat too rapidly or not at all. This danger can be overcome by careful supervision of the program.

A Representative Program

The Hughes High School (Cincinnati, Ohio) has a well-organized program of intramural activities. Although the school is severely lacking in facilities, it offers a broad and varied program that attracts widespread student participation. The following description of the program is based on a mimeographed account written by the director, Howard L. Grimes.[19]

The program is organized and administered by a faculty director with the aid of student assistants. His job is one of guidance and supervision. The faculty director is assisted by an intramural manager, two assistant intramural managers, a record manager, a points award manager, an equipment manager, and team captains—all students.

The intramural manager is responsible for entering teams or individuals in each sport. He must notify each team's captain when and where contests will take place and post all scores of previous contests. He must be furnished the names of all players before each scheduled contest in order that they may check their eligibility. The assistant intramural managers assist him in any way possible.

---

[19] Howard L. Grimes, "Hughes High School Experimental Intramural Sports Program" (Cincinnati, Ohio: Cincinnati Public Schools, 1961). Mimeographed.

The record manager must maintain a homeroom record card indicating the numbers of quarters, innings, and so on, participated in by each student. In addition, he must keep all game scorecards on file and transfer this informaton to the appropriate homeroom record card. The points award manager assists the record manager, checks all homeroom record cards to determine current intramural leaders, and checks all individual point cards to determine the leading scorer at each level.

The equipment manager is responsible for checking all equipment the day before a game, checking equipment to team captains, and maintaining a written record of all equipment. The team captain is responsible for the appearance of his team at the proper time and place, for filing all protests with the intramural manager, for the conduct of his team on the field, and for checking out all necessary equipment from the equipment manager.

The intramural council is composed of the faculty director, the intramural manager, the assistant intramural managers, the record manager, the points awards manager, the equipment manager, and the team captains. Its duties are to formulate rules and regulations, to determine player eligibility, to judge all protests, and to pass decisions on any cases not covered in the rules and regulations.

The program for junior and senior high school boys includes tennis, flag football, basketball, water polo, table tennis, weight lifting, volleyball, rollerskating, gymnastics, chess and checkers, wrestling, the pentathlon, softball, foul shooting, and a field day.

Official rules are followed in all sports. In some cases, specific rules were adapted to meet the particular situation. This was done in the interest of safety and because of the limited facilities at Hughes. In flag football, for instance, three games are played across the normal football field. The goal line is the side line of the football field. The boundary lines are from end-zone line to the thirty-yard line, from thirty-yard line to thirty-yard line, and from the thirty-yard line to the end-zone line. Nine players make up a team; however, a team may play with fewer men. Kick-offs are made from the goal line of the kicking team. The receiving team may throw a forward pass if the kick receiver catches the ball before it hits the ground and takes no more than two steps. Out-of-bounds kicks are put in play in the middle of the field by the receiving team. Punting is not permitted on kick-offs. All forward passes must be made from

behind the line of scrimmage. Every player is an eligible pass receiver. Blocking is permitted above the waist only, and the blocker
may not make a flying block. Scoring proceeds in a manner similar
to that followed in regulation football.

Touchdown: 6 points
Safety: 2 points
Extra points
   Run: 2 points
   Pass: 1 point

There are no field goals or kicks for extra points. The ball is placed
on the two-yard line for the point after a touchdown. After a safety,
the kick-off is from the goal line. It is interesting to note the rule on
recoveries: any fumbles in a backward direction which hit the
ground may be advanced or recovered only by the offensive team;
any other fumbles are dead at the point of fumble. This is a well-
conceived safety factor. These changes and adaptations are typical
of current practice in the athletic field and reflect sound administrative policies.

All regularly enrolled male students at Hughes High School are
eligible to participate. Any student who has received a varsity letter
in a sport is not eligible to compete in that sport. A player who has
played one game with a team may not change to another team, nor
may he play on more than one team in that sport. An individual
excused from physical education may not compete in intramural
athletics. A physical examination may be required at the discretion
of the intramural director. Any individual absent from school on
the day of a scheduled game may not play in that game.

The players are grouped according to homeroom. A homeroom
may enter as many teams as desired. If one homeroom does not
have enough boys to enter a team, it may combine with another
homeroom to form one. Where possible, a separate league is formed
for each grade level. In every case, the junior and senior high school
teams will play in separate leagues. This type of organization is
effective in producing a maximum number of leagues with a minimum number of teams in each league. Round-robin scheduling is,
therefore, employed whenever possible. Only if time and facilities
are limited are double- or single-elimination tournaments used.

Any protests must be made on the field of play and presented in
writing to the director of intramurals on the day of the game. Both

teams, and the officials as well, may present their version of the situation before a decision is made by a majority vote of the intramural council. If a protest is sustained, the game is replayed from the beginning of the segment in which the protest occurred.

If a team fails to appear at the appointed time, the contest is forfeited to the other team. A shortage of players does not automatically constitute a forfeit unless the shorthanded team does not want to play. A forfeit counts as a loss in the standings. Any team that forfeits twice in a season is eliminated for the rest of the season. If a team is eliminated by reason of forfeit, the remaining games count as wins for their scheduled opponents.

Several different awards are presented annually. The three boys in each grade with the highest cumulative point total for the year receive a trophy. Each boy on a championship team receives a certificate of merit and a felt banner. Each boy on a second-place team receives a red ribbon. Third-place team members receive white ribbons. The eight officials having the highest number of points receive small plaques. Intramural managers also receive plaques.

The awards are based on the following point system:

Each entry: 10 points
Each win: 2 points
Each loss: 1 point
Forfeits: 0 points
Each team championship: 10 points
Second-place team championship: 6 points
Third-place team championship: 3 points
Each individual championship: 6 points
Second-place individual championship: 4 points
Third-place individual championship: 3 points
Each game an official works: 3 points
Being homeroom representative: 10 points
Each meeting attended by homeroom representative: 2 points[20]

Despite limited facilities, the Hughes High School intramural program is an outstanding example of the application of educationally sound policies designed to achieve the objective of "Athletics for All."

---

[20] *Ibid.,* p. 5.

CHAPTER III

The Extramural Athletics Program

Extramural athletics, because they are increasingly utilized by educational institutions at all levels and because they provide students with an informal interschool or intercollege athletic experience, deserve special and separate consideration in any book on athletics. Although many of the facts covered in the chapter on intramural athletics—such as objectives, standards of eligibility, and financial arrangements—are applicable to extramurals, nevertheless, the extramural program is separate and distinct in many significant aspects.

Definition

Extramurals are a phase of the interscholastic or intercollegiate athletic program, in which students from different schools or colleges compete against each other. They include play days, sports days, and invitation meets, which are conducted on an informal basis and emphasize the fun and social experiences that accrue to participants, rather than winning and the recognition of individual champions. There are no spectators, leagues, gate receipts, or other features associated with the more highly organized varsity program.

The extramural athletic program may, in part, grow out of the intramural program. A particular intramural team or group of outstanding players is selected to compete on an informal basis with another team or group of students from another school. Such interscholastic or intercollegiate events may be held periodically throughout the school year or may be scheduled to be held at the end of the intramural season. This practice is popular not only among junior and senior high schools but also among colleges, especially among neighboring colleges where a strong rivalry exists.

Sports day. One form of extramural athletics competition is the sports day. Girls and women have utilized this type of event in

41

many parts of the country and in recent years more boys and men are finding it to be an attractive educational experience. A sports day involves competition among teams from several schools. City and county school systems or colleges often sponsor sports days in which all schools or colleges within the district or city congregate for competition in such sports as basketball, track or field hockey. A sports day may take the form of a districtwide or citywide competition, such as those held in Norfolk, Virginia. Each year Norfolk City Public Schools sponsor citywide physical education demonstrations, swimming meets and competitions in volleyball, bowling, tennis, wrestling, basketball, table tennis, and physical fitness. In a sports day, the contestants may compete under the banner of the school or college in which they are enrolled. When several schools or colleges participate in a sports day, the number of activities may range from one to eight. There are no significant awards for the various events and the publicity is not of a nature that builds up the desire to win.

Play day. A play day, unlike a sports day, involves competition between teams made up of students from different schools or colleges. For example, in a girl's basketball play day, half a dozen schools or colleges may be represented; each team, therefore, would be composed of one player from each of the institutions. Frequently, several activities are presented. A play day emphasizes the social values of participation. The teams usually are identified by uniforms, arm bands, numbers, or other distinctive devices.

Mail and telegraphic meets. Mail and telegraphic meets are another type of extramural competition appropriate for such activities as golf, bowling, track, rifle shooting, and archery. Teams play at their own school and then send their scores to a central location, where a winner is determined.

Invitation meet. An invitation meet may be held for one sport or activity or for many. A school or college may invite a team or teams or group of students from another institution to participate in a particular activity or activities. The event is informal and the emphasis is on the fellowship and fun to be derived from the occasion. The competition is more intense than that which occurs in intramural activity because the students play against students from other schools.

Examples of Extramurals

Examples of college-level extramural athletics exist at Bard College and at the University of Kentucky.

In 1950, Bard College, a small liberal arts college in New York, instituted an extramural series with a neighboring college, the New Paltz State Teachers College of the State University of New York. At the close of each intramural season, the winning intramural teams in several sports in each college compete against the winning teams from the other school. The games are friendly, with no trophies or championships involved. The winning teams alternate in their visits to their opponents' campus. Arrangements are very informal. The respective intramural directors act as the officials. The informal social gatherings held after the games often result in lasting friendships, and the exchange of ideas and common problems is productive for the participants.

At the University of Kentucky, the Women's Athletic Association sponsors extramural teams in basketball, hockey, softball, and tennis. All interested girls are eligible to participate, provided they attend three fourths of the practice sessions.

Some considerations for the organization and conduct of play and sports days and other extramural events are:

1. The details of organization and conduct of the event can be placed in the hands of student leaders, thus providing them with excellent opportunities for learning and experience. In many cases, student committees can handle the details involved in extending invitations, registering players, scheduling activities, presenting awards, providing food and entertainment, and officiating.

2. All students should be involved; no players should be left sitting on the bench.

3. Any sport or recreational activity may be presented, depending on the interests and needs of the students and the availability of equipment and facilities.

4. The number of participants should be as large as possible in light of available space and equipment.

5. Only participants who are medically fit should be permitted to engage in athletic activity.

Here is one way in which a play day might be organized:

Morning

9:00–9:30	Registration
9:30–9:45	Welcome, Instructions, Introductions, and Mixer
9:45–10:00	Dress

10:00–11:00

Volleyball
Red vs. Blue: Court 1
Green vs. Yellow: Court 2
Winners vs. Winners: Court 1
Losers vs. Losers: Court 2

Softball
Brown vs. Pink:
Diamond 1
White vs. Black:
Diamond 2

11:00–12:00

Volleyball
Brown vs. White: Court 1
Pink vs. Black: Court 2
Winners vs. Winners: Court 1
Losers vs. Losers: Court 2

Softball
Red vs. Green:
Diamond 1
Blue vs. Yellow:
Diamond 2

Noon

12:00–12:15	Showers, Dress
12:15–1:15	Luncheon

Afternoon

1:15–1:45	Talks by representatives from various schools
1:45–2:30	Presentation of entertainment and awards
2:30	Farewell

Extramurals and Education

Interscholastic athletics—especially at the junior high school level or Grades 7–9—have been the subject of much discussion in recent years. Some educators maintain that highly organized varsity athletics are appropriate at this educational level; others argue the contrary.

The Southern Association of Colleges and Secondary Schools cites some arguments for those educators who oppose varsity-type athletic programs for the junior high school:

A full measure of physical development and social enjoyment can be secured through a rich intramural program. Competitive sports between schools are simply not essential at the junior high school level. It is more educational to teach the skill in a wide range of activities which can be enjoyed immediately and in future years and yet provide competition in keeping with the developmental level of the participants. . . .[1]

Educators who oppose varsity athletics in the junior high school argue that such competition is made unwholesome by community pressures which carries the danger of injury to the students, is educationally unsound in light of the developmental needs of students, creates undesirable tension, and involves specialization at too early an age.

The extramural athletics program is excellent for the high school and the college, but it is especially appropriate for the junior high school. It offers participants informal games and activities with students from other schools, and competition less highly organized than found in the senior high school. The program fits in well with the students' developmental patterns because it is more competitive than the intramurals offered in the upper grades of the elementary school but less competitive than the varsity-type sports offered at the senior high school and college levels. The intensity of the competition increases gradually, so that the student is not cast abruptly into a situation for which his developmental level, according to many educators, has not equipped him.

Extramural programs are being utilized to an increasing extent in junior high schools as a means of introducing the student to interscholastic athletics, and at the senior high school and college levels as a means of enriching the total athletic offering for all boys and girls.

Some of the general policies recommended by educators for the organization and conduct of the extramural program are:

1. The philosophy and objectives of the extramural program should be consistent with those of general education and of physical education. The program should contribute to the total development of the individual by providing activities that further his social, emotional, mental, and physical development.

2. The supervision of the extramural program should be the responsibility of the director of physical education, who will insure that optimum educational values accrue to the participants.

3. The planning and conduct of the extramural program should

---

[1] The Southern Association of Colleges and Secondary Schools, A Joint Study Conducted by the Commission on Secondary Schools and the Commission on Research and Service. *The Junior High School Program* (Atlanta, 1958).

be based upon democratic principles and provide for the voluntary participation of the entire student body, regardless of skill or ability. The program should serve as a laboratory in which students can utilize the skills learned in required physical education classes.

4. The program may involve sports days, play days, field days, invitational meets, telegraphic meets, and other events which interest students and are of value to them. Some of the events should be conducted on a coeducational basis.

5. The financing of the extramural program should proceed like that of other educational programs of the school or college and all available facilities should be utilized in order to provide for maximum participation.

6. The units of competition should depend upon the size of the school or college, the nature of the activity, the availability of equipment and facilities, the needs and interests of the students, the formation of groups within the school or college, and the availability of staff.

7. Only qualified officials should be used. In most cases this would mean having educational personnel, women officials for girls' and women's activities, and individuals who are well acquainted with the physical, mental, social, and emotional characteristics and needs of the participants.

8. Eligibility requirements should be kept to a minimum and should be designed to protect the health of the participants, insure equality of competition, and encourage the participation of as many students as possible.

9. Achievement in the extramural program may be recognized by some type of award which has no monetary value (so that it does not act as a motive for participation).

10. The students, the faculty, and the general public should be kept informed of the objectives, the policies, and the activities of the extramural program so that their interest is aroused and their understanding assured.

CHAPTER IV

Varsity Interscholastic
and Intercollegiate Athletics

The varsity interscholastic and intercollegiate athletics program represents the apex of the physical education program. Table 4 shows the extent of sports participation in the schools of America. This program is specifically designed to meet the needs of students with outstanding athletic ability. The educationally sound program, however, must include many different activities at many different skill levels in order to insure that challenging competition is provided to meet and satisfy the needs of the greatest number of students.

All the values of athletics cited in Chapter I—physical fitness, individual development, and social development—may accrue to those who participate in the interscholastic and intercollegiate program. Note that participation alone does not guarantee these values. The instilling of educational values depends on the leadership of the program and the application of sound principles in the administration of the program.

Organization and Administration

Structure. Athletic organization takes one of two general forms, of which there may be many variations. Athletics may be organized as an integral part of the physical education structure, or as a separate unit totally unrelated to physical education. Those departments of athletics which operate as separate units have evolved from the nineteenth century, when athletics were not considered an integral part of the curriculum. Such an organization is no longer justified and is certainly not consistent with current educational philosophy, which recognizes the educational value of athletics and considers athletics to be intrinsically related to education.

Whether the athletics program is an integral part of the general structure or a separate unit, the departmental organization is essen-

47

TABLE 4. 1964 SPORTS PARTICIPATION SURVEY.*

Sport	Number of Schools	Number of Participants
Archery	30	175
Badminton	214	1,956
Baseball	13,248	357,145
Basketball	19,112	639,755
Bowling	456	8,220
Cross Country	5,390	101,773
Curling	581	5,393
Decathlon	25	75
Fencing	22	184
Field Hockey	2	40
Football: 11-Man	12,922	772,802
8-Man	1,060	25,240
6-Man	237	4,744
Golf	5,792	62,630
Gymnastics	613	13,091
Hockey	486	11,665
Lacrosse	59	1,500
One-Mile Team Race	105	840
Pentathlon	55	130
Riflery	270	4,120
Rowing	101	505
Rugby	10	192
Rugger	23	390
Skiing	400	6,479
Soccer	1,443	32,506
Softball	348	7,071
Swimming	2,042	60,216
Tennis	5,072	76,368
Track and Feld	15,524	512,271
Track (Indoor)	646	8,322
Volleyball	3,488	44,012
Water Polo	106	4,367
Wrestling	4,237	126,862

* 1964 interscholastic athletic summary of The National Federation of State High School Athletic Associations. Printed in *Sportscope,* IX (July 29, 1964).

tially the same. Most colleges and some schools have some type of athletic board or committee which establishes the athletic policies of the institution. It may be made up entirely of faculty members or it may also include student representatives. Such boards or committees are responsible for the conduct and administration of the interscholastic or intercollegiate athletics program. They also have the responsibility of keeping the whole faculty informed of the athletics situation.

The responsibility for the implementation of the athletic board's policies is delegated to an athletics director. He is really the business manager of the athletics program. His responsibilities include preparing the budget; purchasing all equipment and supplies; providing for proper maintenance and care of the equipment and facilities; preparing all the schedules; obtaining officials for all home games; maintaining records on equipment, eligibility, and awards; arranging for transportation, physical examinations, and insurance; and insuring the smooth and efficient operation of the program as a whole. In larger schools and universities, the director may have a staff to help him, including a business manager and an equipment manager.

In general, however, the importance of integrating the athletics department within the department of physical education cannot be overemphasized. If the interscholastic and intercollegiate athletics programs truly represent the apex of the physical education program, then it is only logical that the organizational structure should reflect this concept.

Leadership. The educational value of athletics which accrues to the participants in the program depend on the quality of the leadership. This leadership depends, in turn, on the coach and the official. Together, these individuals are responsible for determining the value system which will be acquired by the athlete.

In terms of his responsibilities to his players, the coach should display the highest standards of ethical conduct and sportsmanship. His ideals must be strong and not open to compromise. In addition, he should be patient and must be able to recognize and control the dynamic situations which occur during a game or practice session and to resolve them in an educationally sound manner.

Ideally, all coaching should be done by members of the physical education staff. This may not be possible if the physical education staff is small and the athletic program highly diversified. All coaches, however, should be certified teachers of physical education. This is very important. Physical education teachers are better prepared to teach athletics and they are more likely to achieve the necessary cooperation between the athletics program and the physical education program.

Although the coach sets the tone of his team, the official sets the tone of the game. C. D. Henry suggests the following criteria for selecting game officials:

1. Knowledge of the game;
2. Good physical condition;
3. Ability to explain rulings to the players;
4. Respect for players and coaches, with tact to maintain rapport;
5. Ability to cooperate with other officials;
6. Individual courage;
7. Ability to make quick and forceful decisions.[1]

Financing.   At present, numerous sources of funds are used to finance athletics. In the public schools, support is received from two sources: tax revenues and gate receipts. Generally, tax revenues are allotted for the construction and maintenance of facilities and for salaries. Operating expenses—such as those incurred for equipment, officials, insurance, awards, and travel—are met through gate receipts.

In addition, some public schools and most colleges and universities derive revenue from the activity fees paid by each student. The fees cover admission to all home athletic contests and all activities sponsored by the various student organizations. Other sources of revenue include fund-raising drives, school dances, soft-drink concessions and athletic carnivals.

Ideally, the total expense of the athletics program should be met by funds from the school budget. If the athletics program is considered an integral part of the curriculum, it should be financed as other parts of the curriculum are. The Educational Policies Commission has declared that "the complete costs of the athletics program should be paid out of general school funds."[2]

Although nonbudgetary sources of funds are not recommended, it is recognized that they are necessary in order to retain most athletics programs. Nevertheless, it would be desirable for the athletics program to be completely subsidized by schools, colleges or universities, and boards of education. If fees are charged for admission to athletic events, gate receipts should be regarded as a source of revenue for the general education budget.

The Educational Policies Commission reports the following results in one city in which the athletics program was incorporated within the general fund.

---

[1] C. D. Henry, "Needed: Criteria for Selecting Officials," *The Physical Educator,* XVIII (October 1961), 98f.

[2] Educational Policies Commission, *School Athletics* (Washington, D.C.: National Education Association, 1954), p. 66.

1. The high school athletic program was no longer a commercial enterprise dependent on gate receipts.

2. Better health and safety standards were maintained: for instance, it was no longer necessary to play in bad weather.

3. Most big games were played on weekend afternoons, when only students could attend, avoiding unpleasant spectator problems, such as vandalism and rowdyism.

4. Central purchasing resulted in savings, while at the same time assuring all schools equipment of similar quality.

5. Some of the hidden costs of high school attendance, such as athletic fees, are reduced for the student.[3]

Extra pay for coaching. The problem of extra pay for coaching has received considerable attention. Extra pay is a supplementary salary given to teachers with a full teaching load who assume additional responsibilities, such as coaching, dramatics, band and orchestra, intramural athletics, club sponsorship, and so on. Opponents of the concept of extra pay argue that the teacher, as a member of a profession, should be guided by his dedication to public service rather than by the desire for personal gain. They conclude that it is not professional to be compensated on a "piecework" basis. Furthermore, they point out that many extra-pay schedules are arbitrary and tend to favor coaches over other teachers with after-school responsibilities.

Those favoring extra pay argue that teachers are not paid professional-level salaries and that most teachers, especially those with family responsibilities, find it necessary to seek additional sources of income. They add that, with the present need for graduate credits to achieve salary increases and the numerous opportunities for tutoring, many teachers cannot afford to accept coaching or other after-school responsibilities without extra pay. They point out that an objective approach to the extra-pay schedule involving all after-school activities is both desirable and possible.

The solution to this problem must be based on the assumption that responsibility for after-school activities does, indeed, make additional demands on a teacher's time which may lead to inefficient teaching. All activities under the guidance of the school, including those not of an academic nature, must be considered as an integral

---
[3] *Ibid.*

part of the curriculum. As a result, the assignment of responsibility for these activities should be considered part of the teaching load. Therefore, if all teachers are to have equal teaching loads, those with afterschool responsibilities should be relieved of duties during the school day. This practice, commonly known as "released time," is consistent with the concept of teaching as a profession and with the desire of administrators to have a single salary schedule.

Snyder has suggested the following plan for implementing such a philosophy:

1. Identify those activities of a nonacademic nature and rate them, using the criteria of time spent and nature of responsibility.

2. Rate the instructional classes (using the same criteria).

3. Use the total of instructional and nonacademic activities to determine the number of faculty members required to carry out the school program; use recommended standards to determine effective teaching loads.

4. Distribute any other responsibilities equitably among faculty members in a manner consistent with personal and professional characteristics.

5. Assign, to all teachers with after-school duties, released time during the morning to be used at their discretion.

6. Study all regularly scheduled after-school activities to determine whether they could be scheduled during the normal school day.[4]

This plan provides opportunities for effective teaching, a fair and equal distribution of the teaching load, an equitable salary scale for all teachers, and possibilities for assigning high ratings to those activities carrying a greater responsibility. This plan has the greatest merit, from a professional standpoint. Some administrators, however, feel that such a plan is not practical because it requires the employment of additional teachers. These administrators argue that, at a time when the supply of good teachers is limited, it is more desirable to pay higher salaries and salary supplements to good teachers who will accept added responsibilities. They also feel that, in the long run, the extra-pay plan is less costly than the released-time plan.

---

[4] Raymond A. Snyder, "The Crucial Issue in the Extra-Pay Controversy," *The Physical Educator,* XVI (May 1959), 62–64.

The alternative, an extra-pay schedule for extra services, may prove satisfactory to all members of the faculty. In practice, the most successful systems are those in which the schedule is set by a faculty committee, composed of administrators; representatives of the departments of athletics, music, dramatics, and physical education; and sponsors of other after-school activities. This committee must identify all after-school activities, rate each position according to some established criteria, and then assign a dollar value to the faculty services involved.

The Roslyn Public Schools (Long Island, New York) devised an extra-pay scale according to this plan; it may serve as a model for other interested faculties. After identifying the activities and positions to be considered, the committee established nine criteria for rating activities. Each criterion was assigned a value of from 1 to 4, indicating its importance:[5]

1. Hours involved   4
2. Number of students   2
3. Experience necessary   2
4. Spectator pressure   2
5. Degree of injury possibility   2
6. Weekend, after-school, or vacation time required   3
7. Equipment and facility responsibility   2
8. Indoor and outdoor environmental factors   1
9. Travel and bus supervision   2

Each position (such as head varsity football coach) was rated from 1 to 5 for each criterion by the committee. This rating was multiplied by the weighted score for that criterion. The sum of these products for each criterion was compiled. The extra-pay rate was established by multiplying the number of points by $10.00.[6] For example, the sum of the product for each criterion for head varsity football coach was 81. Therefore, the rate of pay was 81 × $10.00, or $810.[7]

The Moses Lake School District (Washington) used six criteria in establishing its pay schedule. Maximum point values for each

[5] Jack George, "Extra Pay for Extra Services," *Administration of High School Athletics* (Washington, D.C.: American Association for Health, Physical Education, and Recreation, 1963), p. 63.

[6] *Ibid.*, p. 61.

[7] *Ibid.*, p. 62.

criterion were established. This had the effect of weighting each factor. The criteria used, with their corresponding maximum point values, were the following:

1. Importance to the students   20
2. Basic responsibilities involved   20
3. Extra time over and above classroom teaching
    and preparation   20
4. Community pressure   20
5. Special training required   10
6. Number of participants   5

The total point value for each position was multiplied by $9.00 to arrive at the extra-pay rate for each position.[8]

It should be noted that, in both plans, objective criteria were established to analyze each position. Each criterion was given a weighted value according to the importance of that criterion; point values were totaled and multiplied by a dollars-per-point figure. To determine the dollar value per point, add the point totals for all positions and divide the amount of money budgeted for after-school activities by this total.

Medical examination.   Most states require that a student pass a physical examination before competing in athletics. Some states require a separate examination for each sport; others require only one for the whole year. A number of states also require that students present a statement granting parental permission to participate in athletics.

In a few cases, the state high school athletic association distributes standard forms or prescribes those items which should be considered a necessary part of the physical examination. Those items which are generally recommended include mention of any significant past illness or injury; height; weight; examination of eyes, ears, nose, throat, lungs, heart, blood pressure, abdomen, genitalia, hernias, reflexes, urinalysis, and blood count or X-ray (if indicated); immunization record for polio and tetanus. In addition, the doctor is asked to cross out (on the list provided) any activities in which the student is not physically able to compete.

A physical examination of this scope is certainly a desirable requirement for participation in all school athletics. It is a necessary

---

8 "Activity Extra-Pay Schedule," Moses Lake School District, Moses Lake, Washington. Mimeographed.

PARENT'S WAIVER

To whom it may concern:

............................19......

I, ... parent
guardian

of .... hereby give my consent for him to train for and compete on the athletic teams of .... High School assuming for myself full responsibility should any accident occur to him either in training for such competition or in the competition itself, or in transportation to or from the place where he may be practicing or playing.

Signed ....

Address ....

SCHOOL PHYSICIAN'S CERTIFICATE

I, ... a physician duly licensed to practice medicine in State of New York, residing at .... do certify that on the ..... day of .... 19....., I examined .... a pupil of the .... High School, and certify that in my judgment he is physically able to train and compete on the athletic teams of the High School.

Signed ....

APPLICATION TO PARTICIPATE IN ATHLETICS

To whom it may concern:

I, ... a pupil in the .... High School, hereby apply for permission to train for and compete in interscholastic athletics of said school and will assume all responsibility for personal injury in training for such competition, in the competition itself or transportation to and from the place of practice or game.

....
Student

....
Date

requirement, preferably on a seasonal basis, for participation in interscholastic or intercollegiate athletics.

Accident insurance. The trend in recent years has been to provide accident insurance for athletes. This trend is based upon the schools' recognition of the dangers inherent in an athletic program and of their moral responsibility to the participants (even though participation is voluntary). The National Federation of State High School Athletic Associations has encouraged this trend in the high schools. Insurance may or may not be sponsored by the state athletic association and it may or may not be paid by the school out of the

---

N. Y. S. H. S. ATHLETIC PROTECTION PLAN
PHYSICAL EXAMINATION CARD FOR SCHOOL YEAR
EXAMINATION GIVEN AT BEGINNING OF EACH SPORT SEASON

Name *........................ School ....

Date of Birth .... Grade .... Weight .... Height ....
*IS THERE HISTORY OF   Fractures: Allergy:
Heart Disease: Dislocation: Complicated .... Antibiotics ....
  Congenital .... Knee Cartilage.... Uncomplicated.... Pollens   ....
  Acquired   .... Other Joints ....Lung Disease .... Drugs   ....
Hernia .... Operations   ....Kidney Disease ....Tetanus Inj. ....
Blood dyscrasia (bleeder) ....

---

*PHYSICAL EXAMINATION (N—Normal)   (P—Pathology)
Summary of positive findings to be explained on reverse side.
Eyes (N)   R... L...Blood pressure—   Hernia   ....
                           systolic ....
  Glasses   R... L...   diastolic ....Orthopedic   ....
  Con. lens   R... L...Normal heart rate ....Extremities   ....
Ears hearing R... L...Rate after exercise ....Abnormalities   ....
  Chronic discharge ....Test (25 hops on 1 foot) Urinalysis recommended
Lungs.... Abdomen....Rate after 2 min. rest.... for albumin & sugar ....
Indicate any known congenital defects ....
DENTAL: List any dental abnormalities ....
*IF SUSPECTED PATHOLOGY EXISTS, FURTHER CONSULTATION AND WORK-UP
  REQUIRED
The above examination shows satisfactory condition to engage in:
Name of Sport   ....
Date of Exam.   ....
                      Fall   Winter   Spring
Signature of School Physician   ....
       This Card to Be Retained in School's Cumulative Health Record File
FORM PE 75M 11-62

general fund. This varies from state to state and within each state. In some instances players are required to pay for their own insurance.

The coverage provided by various state and independent plans is essentially the same. Minimum coverage includes benefits for accidental death or dismemberment, hospital expenses, surgical and dental expenses, X ray fees, and physicians' fees. Benefits for death and dismemberment range from five hundred to one thousand dollars. For hospital expenses, the range is from seven to eight dollars per day for ten to thirty days. Surgical benefits vary according to the extent of the injury; the maximum is three hundred dollars. Dental benefits may or may not be included in the schedule of surgical benefits; they range from fifteen to twenty-five dollars for one tooth and from thirty to fifty dollars for two or more teeth. X ray benefits vary from ten to fifteen dollars. Physicians' benefits are paid in cases when an accident does not require hospitalization, but does require a doctor's care. The benefits payable vary from two to three dollars per visit, up to a maximum of fifteen to thirty dollars. In some plans, catastrophe benefits are also available for injuries requiring extensive medical care and long-term hospitalization. Coverage is normally provided on a deductible basis, with the insurance company paying 75–80 per cent of the total cost over the deductible amount up to a maximum of from 2500 to 3500 dollars.

Eligibilty. One of the most important contributions of the various national, state, and local athletic conferences and associations is the development of eligibility regulations. In many cases, the enforcement of these regulations has minimized the many abuses which were so rampant in school sports before the turn of the century. High school and college regulations, because of their nature, must be treated separately. Current practices in interscholastic athletics include regulations relating to age, semesters in school, enrollment, scholarship, amateur status, independent team participation, transfer, recruiting, and awards.

The age limit in most states is now nineteen. Generally, a student is ineligible to play in a given year if his nineteenth birthday occurs before September 1st of that year. In some cases, a boy is ineligible to play in those seasons which begin after his nineteenth birthday. The important point is the downward trend in age requirements: twenty was formerly accepted as the maximum age for participation, but in recent years the majority of states have reduced that maximum by one year. This trend is in keeping with the trend to earlier graduation from high school. In effect, then, the lower age limit is successful in insuring more equal competition.

Another accepted rule is that a student who has been enrolled for eight semesters in Grades 9–12 is ineligible for further competition. In addition, the seventh and eighth semesters must be consecutive; a student enrolled in a fifth fall or spring semester is not eligible to play. Attendance for a period ranging from ten days to three weeks or more constitutes a semester's attendance under this rule.

To be eligible to compete in athletics, the student must be enrolled in the school for the semester in which competition is to occur, and he must be in regular attendance. Most states set a deadline, sometime within the first three to four weeks of a semester, within which a person must enroll in order to be eligible. In Washington, students must be enrolled not later than October 1st to be eligible during the first semester, and by February 15th to be eligible for the second semester.[9] In Texas, a student must be in regular attendance from the first day of the second week of a school year, and/or he must be in regular attendance at the school he represents for a thirty-day period immediately preceding the contest.[10] Furthermore, most states require that a student must have been in regular attendance at some junior or senior high school during the preceding semester.

Two general regulations, which have almost universal application, govern scholarship. First, a student must have a passing average in at least fifteen hours of academic work. This would be the equivalent of three daily one-hour courses. The average is determined on a cumulative basis from the beginning of each semester. Secondly, a student must have passed fifteen hours of work per week in the semester immediately preceding that in which he desires to participate.

The amateur rule also has universal application, but many different definitions and criteria are employed in the various states. The

9 Washington Interscholastic Activities Association, *Handbook, 1963–1964* (Seattle: Washington Interscholastic Activities Association), p. 40.

10 Unversity Interscholastic League, *Constitution and Contest Rules of the University Interscholastic League for 1962–1963* (Austin, Tex.: The University of Texas), p. 19.

rule recommended by the National Federation of State High School Athletic Associations considers a student ineligible for amateur standing if:

1. He has accepted remuneration for participating in an athletic contest;
2. He has participated under an assumed name;
3. He has competed on a team with players who were paid for their participation;
4. He has signed a contract with a professional team or agent.[11]

The principles and policies of the Washington Interscholastic Activities Association are representative of those in effect throughout the nation.

> He [the student] shall be an amateur as defined by the National Collegiate Athletic Association as follows: "An amateur student-athlete is one who engages in athletics for the physical, mental, social, and educational benefits he derives therefrom, and to whom athletics is an avocation."
>
> For an individual to lose his amateur standing, he must commit one of the following acts:
>
> 1. Enters a competition for money or for prizes of more than thirty-five dollars in value;
> 2. Sells or pawns his prize;
> 3. Accepts a purse of money;
> 4. Enters a competition under a false name;
> 5. Teaches, trains, or coaches in an athletic sport for money or any valuable consideration;
> 6. Accepts payment of excessive expense allowance: it shall be permissible to provide only actual and necessary expenses on athletic trips; it is not permissible to pay money to team members for unspecified or unitemized items;
> 7. Signs or has ever signed a contract to play professional athletics (whether for a money consideration or not); plays or has ever played on any professional team in any sport; receives or has ever received, directly or indirectly, a salary or any other form of financial assistance (including scholarships or educational grants-in-aid) from a professional sports organization or any of his expenses for reporting to or visiting a professional team.
>
> A student athlete may:
>
> 1. Participate as an individual or as a member of a team against professional athletes, but he may not participate on a professional

[11] The National Federation of State High School Athletic Associations, *Handbook, 1960–1961* (Chicago: The National Federation of State High School Athletic Associations), p. 12.

team. He may play summer baseball as an amateur on any team not under the jurisdiction of professional baseball, provided it meets the foregoing definition and he does not receive pay for participation.

2. Be employed in the intramural sports program of his institution and his duties may include officiating of intramural contests at the going rate for such employment. He may not officiate for compensation in athletic contests outside his institution.

3. Work as a counselor in a summer camp, life guard, swimming pool attendant, and swimming instructor for children or groups of children without affecting his eligibility under the terms of this principle; he may work in a tennis or golf shop provided he does not give instruction for compensation, and he may obtain employment with a recreation department, his duties to include some officiating and coaching responsibilities; however, he may not be employed as an athletic coach.[12]

Normally, a high school student may not play on any other team in the same sport after he has played a game for the school team he represents. For example, a boy could not play on the school team and also on the YMCA team. The West Virginia Secondary School Activities Commission has the following rule relative to limited team membership:

> After a student has become a member of a senior or junior high school team and has represented his school in a contest, he may play only upon his school team for the remainder of that season. If he plays with another team not concerned with the school, he is ineligible for further participation upon his school team for that season in that particular sport.[13]

Rules pertaining to transfer students are similar in all states. A student whose parents or legal guardians move into a new school district maintains the same eligibility he had at his previous school. If, however, the application of undue influence can be proved, the student is ineligible to play in the school to which he transfers. *Undue influence* is defined as "an act by any person or group connected with a school or not connected with a school to persuade a student to enroll in an out-of-zone school or to persuade his parents or guardians to move to the zone of another school."[14] The rule per-

[12] Washington Interscholastic Activities Association, *op. cit.,* p. 41f.

[13] West Virginia Secondary School Activities Commission, *Handbook, 1962* (Parkersburg, W.Va.: The Board of Appeals of The West Virginia Secondary School Activities Commission), p. 27.

[14] *Ibid.*

taining to undue influence has been added in recent years in order to prevent the recruiting of athletes and to reserve team membership for those who legitimately live in a district.

Most states have set a limit on the dollar value of athletic awards. The following rule from West Virginia is typical:

> Any student who accepts any medal, cup, trophy, or other award of any kind having a value of more than three dollars, except the unattached letter awarded by his school, either as a direct or indirect compensation for athletic knowledge, or skill in consequences of being on an athletic team shall immediately be ineligible for any interscholastic contest.[15]

College eligibility requirements pertain to residence and undergraduate status, transfer, scholastic average, limits of participation, and amateur status. In general, a student must be in residence at the college or university one full year, and he must be fully matriculated and registered as a candidate for a degree before he is eligible for varsity competition. (There are exceptions to this rule, depending on the male population of the school: in some schools, freshman students are eligible for varsity competition.) In order to fulfill the requirements for residence and undergraduate status, a student must be carrying a full program, as defined by the rules and regulations of the college in which he is enrolled. A transfer student is not eligible during his first year of residence. (Transfer students in junior colleges, however, do not come under the one-year residence requirement.) Furthermore, a student must be making normal quantitative progress toward the completion of his degree requirements and he must have a satisfactory cumulative grade average—i.e., one which is not substantially below the over-all cumulative grade average required for a bachelor's degree in the college program in which he is enrolled. A student is limited to one year of participation as a freshman athlete and three years as a varsity athlete. In addition, no student may participate after the expiration of four consecutive twelve-month periods following the date of his initial enrollment in a college or university. Also, a student must maintain his amateur status according to the same standards applied to interscholastic athletics.

Recruiting. Recruiting has been the bane of college athletics—

---

[15] *Ibid.,* p. 28.

and, to some extent, of high school athletics—since the nineteenth century. Only in recent years has high school recruiting been cut to a minimum with the passing of eligibility regulations governing transfers and undue influence to transfer. College recruiting abuses, although tempered by strict association legislation, continue. Men with broad experience in the administration of college athletics agree that recruitment is the major problem in college athletics. Unfortunately, college recruiting practices also have a pronounced effect on high schools.

Eugene Youngert cites two cases of distorted bidding in his article on the pressures exerted upon high schools by college athletics. In the first case, a high school football player who had received twenty-six scholarship offers to play football in college received a telegram from a leading college football team which said: "Accept no offers until you see ours."[16] In another case, a high school principal received a letter from an interested college saying:

> We should like to have the boy come to our campus for a week-end and get the feel of our athletic facilities. If you will bring him to us, we will invite you and your wife, your athletic director and his wife, and the boy's mother and father to spend the weekend here as our guests. We shall provide first-class transportation and campus hospitality.[17]

The athlete's sense of values cannot help but be distorted by such abusive practices, not to mention the values of other students, who see greater awards bestowed on athletic prowess than on scholastic achievement. This is particularly true when college admissions are so highly competitive.

As a guide to the prospective college athlete, the Eastern College Athletic Conference has called attention to the following excessive practices of overeager recruiters:

1. Excessive entertainment. . . .
2. Excessive persistence, involving too many representatives of a single college, and too many and too frequent contacts.
3. Wetnursing a candidate through the application stages, handling all his relations for him with the admissions and financial aid offices, going far beyond what is done for nonathletes, and in effect doing his thinking for him.

---

16 Eugene Youngert, "College Athletics, Their Pressure on the High Schools," *The Atlantic Monthly,* CCII (October 1958), 36.
17 *Ibid.*

4. Suggestions, veiled or open, of privately provided financial aid, or "fringe benefits," such as holiday transportation, over and above what the college will provide under its own and ECAC and NCAA rules.

5. Indications that the recruiter's interest in him is based chiefly on his athletic promise, with only casual attention to his scholastic ability and aims, his seriousness of purpose, and his personal character.[18]

The real solution to the recruiting problem is twofold. First, colleges must strictly observe the regulations set up by the NCAA and respective athletic conferences. Secondly, college and university faculties must assume responsibility for and authority over recruiting and admissions procedures.

Various athletic associations have established effective rules and regulations to control recruiting. Most associations have similar laws governing communication with prospective athletes, campus visits, inducements, entertainment, visits to high schools and tryouts.

Communication is allowed with a prospective athlete by letter or telegram, by telephone to his residence, and by personal interview on the college campus. Addresses before an audience which may include a number of athletes is also allowed.

An institution may finance only one visit to its campus for a prospective student, and the visit may not exceed forty-eight hours. A prospective athlete may make additional visits at his own expense. Also, any person—other than a representative of a college or its athletic interests—may transport or pay the transportation costs of a prospective student from his own personal resources, provided he accompanies the prospective student. No institution or its alumni or its friends may finance the transportation of the relatives, friends, or high school coaches of a prospective student to the campus. If several prospective students travel together in the same car, the college may pay the cost of the trip, but it counts as the official paid visit for each of the prospective athletes who makes the trip.

No representative of the athletic interests of a college or university may solicit the attendance of a prospective athlete at his institution with the offer of financial aid or equivalent inducements. Under no circumstances may travel expenses be offered or provided to a prospective student, except in connection with the single cam-

---

[18] Eastern College Athletic Conference, "A Summary of Basic Principles and Rules Regarding Financial Aid." New York, leaflet.

pus visit. This rule would pertain to travel expenses to and from college, during vacation periods, and to or from a summer job.

A college or university may not arrange for or permit excessive entertainment of a prospective student. Any entertainment is limited to admission to events held on the college campus or to local events which are approved for all university students. Transportation of an athlete or members of his family to a site other than the college campus and community or the student's hometown area is not permitted.

A representative of a college or university may not visit a high school except as part of a regularly scheduled, publicized event. Some conferences will allow a college representative to visit a prospective student at his high school if the representative has obtained official permission from the school principal.

An institution may not conduct, or have conducted in its behalf, any athletic practice session, test, or coaching school at which prospective students display their abilities in any sport.

The foregoing regulations, which are designed to prevent those abuses which detract from the educational values of athletics, can be effective only if they are enforced by their respective associations and if they are honored by member colleges and universities. The enforcement of regulations has been increased by the athletic associations with the authority to do so; however, the responsibility for honoring these regulations within the institutions themselves must lie with the faculties. Historically, the faculties of many colleges and universities ignored the athletic program of the institution. Yet the college faculty represents the one body which is capable of enforcing these regulations within the college: its authority lies in two primary areas: admissions and scholarship aid. The faculty is in a good position to demand that all prospective students be evaluated on the same academic standards and that no substandard admissions be permitted. The faculty should also demand that scholarships be granted on the basis of financial need to those students who have exhibited a high aptitude for college work at recommended academic levels. The following recommendations might well be adopted as policies at all colleges and universities:

1. Financial aid—whether it be in the form of scholarships, grants, loans, or jobs—should be administered by the same agency for all students of a college or university.

2. The recipient of such aid should be given a written statement of the amount, duration, and conditions of the award.

3. All recipients of financial aid should be admitted on the same basis and required to maintain the same standards as all other students.

4. The awarding of financial aid must be based on well-established financial need or high scholarship. The standards for judging financial need and/or high scholarship should be the same for all students.

5. In regard to employment, the rate of pay for all students who do the same or similar jobs, must be the same.

6. Under no circumstances may a student be deprived of financial aid, once the award has been confirmed in writing, because of failure to participate in intercollegiate athletics.

Awards. The policy of granting awards has been the subject of a great deal of discussion. Educators have long felt that the true rewards of athletic competition are the physical and psychological values which accrue to the participant. They have also recognized that it is traditional in our society for winners to be presented some evidence of their success. This dichotomy has been resolved in recent years by the trend toward minimizing the material value of the award. The athletic award has become a symbol of the real rewards of competition. This philosophy is manifest in the many state rules limiting the dollar value of athletic awards.

Another recent trend has been the abolition of any discrimination between "major" and "minor" sports in the granting of athletic awards. In former years, it was common practice to have separate awards for "major" sports—football, basketball, baseball, and track —and "minor" sports—soccer, cross-country, tennis, golf, swimming, and wrestling. This practice was based on the philosophy that those participating in the "major" sports were making a greater contribution to the school than those participating in the "minor" sports, and should, therefore, receive an award of greater value. This type of thinking went out with the acceptance of athletics as an integral part of the curriculum. Participation in any athletic competition— no matter what the sport—yields desirable educational values. As such, all sports must be treated equally and their participants must receive the same awards.

In the granting of athletic awards, the emphasis has been placed, not on the quality of the participation, but on its extent. If awards are truly symbolic of the values received from competition, then the amount of participation must be the determining factor in establishing eligibility for an award. The following requirements for earning a letter at the Moses Lake High School (Washington) reflect this basic philosophy. The 175 points required to earn a letter may be earned in different ways in different sports. In all cases, a student participating in a sport for a full season receives forty-five service points. These are cumulative from year to year for those boys who do not otherwise qualify for a letter. The required total may also be earned in the following ways:

Baseball   for each meet: 12 points
             for first place: 5 points
             for second place: 3 points
             for third place: 2 points
             for fourth place: 1 point

Basketball   for each quarter of a nonconference game: 2 points
             for each quarter of a conference game: 4 points

Football   for each quarter of play: 7 points

Wrestling   for each match: 12 points
             for each pin: 5 points
             for each decision: 3 points
             for each draw: 2 points[19]

It is common practice to differentiate between varsity awards and junior varsity or freshman awards. This may be done by giving different-sized letters or by indicating on the letter the type of award it represents. It is also common to differentiate between the first letter in a varsity sport and subsequent awards in the same sport. Many schools give chevron stripes or bars to be worn on the sleeve of the letter sweater. Others give different awards, such as miniature footballs or keys. Still others give a certificate indicating that a student has won a second or third award in the same sport. Whatever the policy, it is well to keep in mind the basic philosophy: namely, that the true rewards of competition come from participation and that the athletic award is simply a symbol of those values.

------

[19] Moses Lake High School, "Requirements for Earning a Letter," Moses Lake School District, Moses Lake, Washington. Mimeographed.

A Representative Program

The Parma Public Schools[20] (Ohio) have a well-organized, efficient, interscholastic athletic administration. The outstanding organization of the athletic program is largely the responsibility of Rex B. Smith, Director of Athletics, Physical Education and Recreation, and his staff. The *Athletic Department Handbook* of the Parma Public Schools, from which much of the following information has been taken, is a thorough, well-conceived statement of athletic policy and administration.

There are two high schools and four junior high schools in Parma. The interscholastic athletics program is administered by a citywide athletic council composed of the Superintendent of the Parma Public Schools; the principals of all secondary schools; the Director of Athletics, Physical Education, and Recreation, of the Parma Public Schools; the faculty managers of athletics of all secondary schools; the heads of the departments of physical education of all secondary schools; and the stadium manager.

The duties of the council are to control and regulate athletics; to evaluate continuously the athletics program; to unify coaching objectives; to adapt policies and procedures designed to meet the highest standards of safety and protection from harmful practices; to direct athletics according to conference, state, and national rules and regulations; to maintain the integration of the athletic program within the physical education program and the educational program in general; and to act in an advisory capacity in the preparation of the budget.

The operational procedures of the council are well defined. The chairman of the council is the Director of Athletics, Physical Education, and Recreation. The procedure for establishing policies and reaching decisions requires that a consensus be reached; if it is not, the proposal is tabled for further discussion at a later date. If a consensus is still not reached, majority and minority reports are filed with the Superintendent of Schools for his final decision. No more than two members of the council may be absent from a meeting in which policy decisions are made.

---

[20] Department of Athletics, Physical Education, and Recreation, *Athletic Department Handbook* (Parma, Ohio: Parma Public Schools), pp. 17–18. Mimeographed.

There are two lines of authority by which the Superintendent of Schools exercises control over the athletics program in Parma. First, the Director of Athletics, Physical Education, and Recreation, is directly responsible to the Superintendent. His function is more supervisory in nature and, therefore, may be considered a staff assignment: he directs and coordinates all the activities of his department; approves athletic contests before they are contracted; prepares the citywide athletic budget; provides specifications and issues purchase orders for athletic supplies and equipment; insures that all rules and regulations of state and local athletic associations are honored; coordinates transportation, equipment care and maintenance, and medical examinations. The second line of control is through the secondary school principal, who is held ultimately responsible for all matters pertaining to the interscholastic athletic program at his school.

The function of the faculty manager of athletics at each school corresponds to that of the director of athletics. The manager, in addition to being a member of the athletic council, must prepare all game contracts; arrange for scorers, timers, judges, and officials for all contests; arrange for physical examinations and insurance and handle the processing of medical claims; maintain records of game contracts, officials' contracts, physical examinations, eligibility information, and medical insurance reports; plan and coordinate all necessary arrangements for each home game; and order and present all letter awards.

The head coach of each sport is responsible for all matters pertaining to the organization and administration of the coaching of the team under his direction. His responsibilities include assigning duties to all assistant coaches; planning and conducting all practice sessions; being responsible for public information releases regarding his sport; cooperating with the faculty manager regarding physical examination schedules; inspecting, issuing, and collecting all equipment and maintaining equipment inventory records; preparing equipment and supply requests to be submitted to the Director of Athletics; recommending letter winners to the faculty manager; recommending to the faculty manager teams that may be scheduled and officials to be employed; and reporting all injuries to the proper school authorities.

Both high schools in Parma offer the same interscholastic program of activities: football, basketball, baseball, track, cross-country, wrestling, tennis, golf, and bowling.

The athletics program is financed through a special athletic department account. All revenues from the sale of tickets, passes, programs, state tournament reimbursements, and other sources of revenue are deposited to this account according to the established budget. All purchasing is done by the Director of Athletics at bid prices. The faculty manager of each school must submit a budget request accompanied by a detailed inventory of the equipment and supplies on hand. The request should include all expenses to be incurred by an individual school for officials, transportation, league expenses, and so on. The budget requests are presented to the Athletic Council by the Director of Athletics. Purchases of an emergency nature may be authorized by the Director of Athletics, subject to formal approval of the Athletic Council at the next regularly scheduled meeting.

The award policy is based on a point total requirement. To meet the requirements for a varsity or junior varsity award, an athlete must have a total of five hundred points. He may earn fifty points for conscientious attendance at practice and games, and fifty points for conscientious training and general conduct. A player who does not receive any points for training and conduct may not receive a letter. The remaining points of the general requirement may be earned as follows:

Baseball (20 games)	for each inning played: 10 points
Basketball (18 games)	for each quarter played: 15 points
Bowling (20 matches of 3 games each)	for each game bowled: 15 points
Cross-Country (12 meets)	for first four places in dual, triangular or quad: 75 points
	for next three places in dual, triangular or quad: 50 points
	for first seven places in major championships (four teams or more): 150 points
Football (10 games)	for each quarter played: 25 points
Golf (14 matches)	for each match played: 75 points
Tennis (20 matches)	for each match played fall and spring: 50 points

| Track (25 meets, indoor and outdoor season) | for each point scored in major championships: 100 points (relay-team members receive one quarter of the total points won by the team) |
| Wrestling (14 matches) | for each dual match participated: 75 points for each dual match won: 25 points for place 1-2-3-4 in a State Tournament: 200 points |

At Parma High School the awards vary for successive letters in the same sport. The first-year award is an eight-inch letter; the second-year award, a gold tieclasp with a school symbol attached; the third-year award, a plaque. In each case, a certificate accompanies the award. The junior varsity award consists of four-inch numerals and a certificate.

In addition, the Parma Athletic Council has established written policies relative to coaches' attendance at clinics; the coaching staff uniforms; the public relations responsibilities of the coaching staff; safety procedures in athletics; procedure in case of injury; number of officials and field doctors and their rates of pay; insurance for participants; the length of sports seasons and the number of contests permitted; the length and organization of practice sessions; transportation and team trips; and game management procedures, such as tickets and admission prices, student responsibilities, permission for broadcasting and television rights, postponed games, concessions, cheerleaders, and bands.

The success of the Parma School System in providing a well-organized interscholastic athletic program is evident from the foregoing discussion of the organization and administration of the program. This success reflects an awareness of some of the problems in the chaotic history of athletics in the schools and a desire to implement some of the lessons of history cited in Chapter I:

1. To accept full responsibility and authority for the athletic program.
2. To live up to the rules and regulations of their respective local, state and national athletic associations.
3. To educate the public to the values inherent in athletics.

CHAPTER V

Girls' and Women's Athletics

Girls' and women's athletics have been a subject of much controversy in recent years. Competitive athletics for boys and men at the senior high school and college levels has had general support and is seldom questioned, but educators of both sexes question the value of such activity for girls and women. Those persons who oppose athletics for girls and women usually do not do so on the basis of medical facts; rather, they ask: "Do athletics contribute to femininity and the position that American women hold in our society?"

The athletic successes of women from other countries, as reflected in Olympic competition, has resulted in a renewed desire on the part of many educators and public-minded citizens to stress sports for the gifted women athletes. The trend would appear to be in the direction of providing more opportunities for girls and women to participate in school and college competitive sports.

Arguments Pro and Con

Some of the arguments against girls' and women's athletics, especially of a highly competitive nature, may be summarized as follows:

1. Athletics for girls should stress those activities which are offered in a broad intramural program. Any interschool athletics should stress the social aspects of athletic competition rather than the development of varsity teams and highly skilled players.

2. Interschool athletics for girls should be limited to extramurals and informal competition, such as play days, sports days, and invitational meets. There should be an emphasis on having fun rather than on winning a school championship or staging a show for spectators.

3. The athletically gifted girl should not be a major concern of physical education leaders. There are too many poorly skilled girls and women that need attention first. The challenge facing physical

educators today is to provide a sound sports program for all girls and women.

4. The social status of girls and women in the American culture is an important consideration. The Olympic champion who puts the shot or throws the discus is not looked upon as reflecting the best image of the American woman. There is no place in highly competitive sports for women who want to reflect the qualities of femininity according to the American standards.

5. The athletics program for girls and women should not duplicate that designed for boys and men. Girls and women have their own special needs and occupy a different role in our society. Therefore, their athletics program should reflect these needs and roles. Furthermore, many of the undesirable practices that have become a part of interscholastic athletics for boys and men must never be permitted to invade the domain of the physical education program for girls and women.

6. There are at present too many pressures upon girls' and women's physical education programs without adding those that would be involved in such things as conditioning and training girls and women for highly organized athletics.

7. Equipment and facilities in schools and colleges are already limited; therefore, it is neither practical nor wise to promote an interschool or intercollegiate athletics program for girls and women. Furthermore, the physical education teacher is already overloaded with classes, intramurals, and other girls' activities. Why add new responsibilities when there isn't enough time now to do those already assigned?

8. High school girls are not sufficiently mature—physically, mentally, or emotionally—to withstand the strains and tensions of highly organized athletic competition.

Some of the arguments that are presented in favor of girls' and women's athletics may be summarized as follows:

1. Sports competition for girls and women, as for boys and men, can develop physical fitness, skills, and desirable social qualities. As long as sports activities are adapted to the girls and their needs, an athletic program will have great value.

2. The highly skilled girl should have the opportunity to compete against other girls of comparable skill. To deny her such a privilege is not educationally sound. Girls and women should have the same

opportunities as boys and men to achieve a high standard of achievement of physical efficiency, skill, and emotional control.

3. Girls and women engage in all sorts of interscholastic and intercollegiate competition such as music festivals, debates, dances, science fairs, and other educational activities. It is also important for them to have the opportunity to compete in a highly organized competitive sports program.

4. If girls and women are denied the right to participate and utilize their superior skill in a school or college sports program, they may seek to utilize this skill in other situations which may be highly undesirable. For example, they may be induced to play with teams that gamble on the outcome of the game, with organizations that do not supply adequate protective equipment, or with individuals of questionable character. The school and college have the responsibility to provide a program for gifted girls and women so that they will not have to look elsewhere.

5. If a highly organized program of athletics for skilled girls and women is administered and conducted by women leaders of physical education, it can have many values for the participants. It is not the competition itself that is harmful; the type of leadership that is provided will determine whether or not the activity has value.

6. A desirable program of varsity sports for girls and women can be provided if the coaches and officials are women; if the competition is in selected sports such as tennis, badminton, golf, archery, and bowling; and the standards of play are established by women.

7. Athletics will provide girls and women with an incentive to achieve a high degree of skill and emotional control; a high level of performance, poise, health, and appearance; and a greater interest in the over-all physical education program.

8. This is a highly competitive world, and women as well as men have to compete. Athletics provide a good training ground for such competition.

Although there are wide differences of opinion concerning athletics for girls and women, there also seems to be some agreement that in any type of athletics program for girls and women—intramural, extramural, or varsity—special consideration must be made for the participants. The program cannot be a duplication of boys and men's athletics. There is also strong support for the idea of having women responsible for the administration, coaching, officiating, and conduct of the athletics program.

Although girls or women may not, because of certain biological factors, ever achieve some of the physical feats of boys or men, there appears to be little biological damage in athletic competition, except where it might interfere with menstruation and the reproductive functions. Furthermore, this appears to be an individual matter: girls and women react to exercise in different ways. The Educational Policies Commission in their report, *School Athletics* (referred to earlier), cited the fact that medical opinion has recommended that girls and women engage only in mild exercise during the first two days of their menstrual flow, in order to avoid physiological damage. It is also recommended that girls and women should avoid activities involving holding the breath, hard vertical landings, or heavy lifting, because such activities increase abdominal pressures on the floor of the pelvis, which may lead to undesirable effects upon the reproductive organs and on the menstrual flow.

Division of Girls' and Women's Sports

The most influential organization in the area of athletics for girls and women is the Division for Girls and Women's Sports (DGWS) of the American Association for Health, Physical Education, and Recreation (AAHPER). The DGWS is responsible for establishing the standards by which most athletic programs are conducted in schools and colleges throughout the nation.

The DGWS is composed of leaders in the field of physical education and recreation who serve in such organizations as schools, colleges, clubs, recreational agencies, military establishments, and industrial plants.

The purpose of the DGWS include:

1. Promoting desirable sports programs for girls and women;
2. Providing leadership for sports programs;
3. Developing guiding principles and standards for use by people responsible for sport programs including, administrators, leaders, officials, and players;
4. Being on call at all times whenever they can be of help to the profession;
5. Continually evaluating the role of girls and women in sports programs;

6. Furnishing materials and information concerned with such items as rules, teaching techniques, and other material for the benefit of players, officials, and sports leaders and teachers.

Some of the DGWS materials include:

a. Official guides in such sports as archery, aquatics, badminton, basketball, bowling, golf, fencing, field hockey, lacrosse, outing activities, riding, soccer, softball, speedball, tennis, track and field, volleyball, and winter sports.

b. Scorebooks in such areas as badminton, basketball, field hockey and volleyball.

c. Special publications, such as pamphlets entitled *Standards in Sports for Girls and Women, The Doctor Answers Some Questions on Menstruation, Recreational Games and Sports, Group Games for Girls and Women, Sports Teaching Materials: Audiovisual Resource List,* and *Special Events in the Girls' Sports Program.*

d. Free fliers, which include *Desirable Practices in Sports for Girls and Women, DGWS At Your Service,* and others.

History. The history of the DGWS goes back about sixty years, when organized sports attracted the interest of many girls and women in sports clubs, recreational agencies, the YWCA, and schools and colleges. (It is interesting to note that a game of basketball was held in 1899 at Smith College.) During these early years there was little attempt to organize and control athletic activities on a national basis. Then, in 1907, *The Women's Basketball Guide* was published. Also, a committee of women was appointed to establish rules for the game. Other attempts to supervise sports occurred in rapid succession following this initial action. In 1916, the American Physical Education Association—now the AAHPER—appointed the Women's Athletic Committee to give some direction to women's sports. This group later became known as the National Section for Women's Athletics and continued to provide leadership for girls and women by preparing guides for various sports, establishing policy, writing rules, and providing consulting and other services. Still later, there developed a larger organization, the National Section for Girls and Women's Sports of the AAHPER. Then, in 1957, the AAHPER invited this group to become a Division for Girls and Women's Sports. This last milestone was an indication of the outstanding growth and value of this organization to the profession.

Another organization that contributed much to the establishment of standards was the Women's Division of the National Amateur Athletic Federation, organized as a private agency in the year 1923.

Other groups, such as the National Joint Committee on Extramural Sports for College Women, have done much to establish standards and procedures for the conduct of tournaments for college women as well as providing outstanding leadership in many other areas of education.

The DGWS—through its publications, consulting services, speakers, and conferences—has spelled out policies and procedures and desirable practices, rules, techniques, and regulations for governing the athletic programs for girls and women in schools and colleges. It has also established standards for the construction of the program, the conduct of the program, the leadership that should be provided, and responsibilities of the participant.

Standards

Some of the standards in sports for girls and women which represent guiding principles in the organization and administration of such programs established by the DGWS are as follows:[1]

The program.   The sports program for girls and women should be developed on the basis of such factors as individual characteristics and needs, individual differences, and the environment surrounding the activity in question.

The leaders of the program should exemplify outstanding physical, mental, social, and emotional traits; possess excellent teaching techniques; be well-informed as to the needs and interests of girls and women; realize that the results of her teaching are enhancing the physical powers and social adjustment of her students.

The participant in the program should assume responsibility for her own health and behavior. The conduct of the sports program should aim to help each player lead and follow according to her merit, skill, willingness, and ability to adapt to the individuals and purposes concerned.

The sports activities should be selected on the basis of the best scientific evidence available and on the contribution such activities can make to the health and welfare of girls and women. Health safeguards should be taken into consideration; the health status of the

---

[1] The Division of Girls and Women's Sports, *Standards in Sports for Girls and Women* (Washington, D.C.: American Association for Health, Physical Education, and Recreation, 1958).

participant should be evaluated and measures provided to adapt the individual's activity and extent of participation to it. The extent to which a girl or woman can participate in athletic activity during the menstrual period should be recognized as an individual matter and proper provisions made.

Competition should be designed to function constructively in the sports program. All players should have the opportunity to participate and compete at their own level of ability. Furthermore, each participant should understand and appreciate the fundamental values that can be gained from participation in a sports program.

Officials should fulfill the qualifications for outstanding leadership —including a consistent and expert knowledge of the girl and the activity.

The rules established by the DGWS are the official rules and should be used.

The leader. The administrator in charge of the sports program for girls and women is responsible for accomplishing the objectives for which the program is established. She has the responsibility for providing a safe, healthful, and desirable physical environment for the conduct of sports activities, and for seeing that the publicity in regard to the sports program is in accordance with the purpose for which the program has been established.

The administrator should hire only properly qualified teachers to conduct the sports program. Teachers should be expert in their task of leading others and understand and utilize the best techniques for teaching and conducting sports. They should reflect all those physical, mental, emotional, and social qualities that they seek to develop in others.

The participant. The participant should develop the desire for participation in accordance with her own individual needs. She should be interested in her own health, in having it periodically appraised by qualified persons, and in engaging in those hygienic practices which reflect such interest.

She should also be interested in developing those skills which will yield satisfaction both in the present and in the future, and should utilize her role in the competitive sports situation wisely and in a manner that yields enjoyment.

Finally, the participant should recognize her responsibility as a cooperative member of the group and her potential as a leader.

Recommendations for Competitive Sports
for Various Age Levels

The recommendations of the DGWS with regard to competitive sports for various age-level groupings form a definitive statement of standards for girls' and women's athletics:

In junior high school, it is desirable that intramural programs of competitive activities be closely integrated with the basic physical education program. Appropriate competition at this level should be comprised of intramural and informal extramural events consistent with social needs and recreational interests. A well-organized and well-conducted sports program should take into account the various skill levels and thus meet the needs of the more highly skilled.

In senior high school, a program of intramural [and] extramural participation should be arranged to augment a sound and inclusive instructional program in physical education. It should be recognized that an interscholastic program will require professional leadership, time, and funds in addition to those provided for the intramural programs. Facilities should be such that the intramural and instructional programs need not be eliminated or seriously curtailed if an interscholastic program is offered.

Specifically, the following standards should prevail:

1. The medical status of the player is ascertained by a physician and the health of the players is carefully supervised.

2. Activities for girls and women are planned to meet their needs, not for the personal glorification of coaches and/or sponsoring organizations.

3. The salary, retention, and promotion of an instructor are not dependent upon the outcome of the games.

4. Qualified women teach, coach, and officiate wherever and whenever possible, and in all cases the professional background and experience of the leaders meet established standards.

5. Rules approved by DGWS are used.

6. Schedules do not exceed the ability and endurance relative to the maturity and physiological conditioning of the participants. Standards for specific sports are defined by DGWS and appear in sports guides, published by the American Association for Health, Physical Education, and Recreation.

7. Sports activities for girls and women are scheduled independently of boys' and men's sports. Exceptions will occur when the activities and/or time and facilities are appropriate for both.

8. Girls and women may participate in appropriate corecreational activities or teams. Girls and women may not participate as members of boys' and men's teams.

9. The program, including health insurance for players, is financed by budgeted school or organization funds rather than entirely by admission charges.

10. Provision is made by the school or organization for safe transportation by bonded carriers, with chaperones who are responsible to the sponsoring group.

In colleges and universities, it is desirable that opportunities be provided for the highly skilled beyond the intramural program. Regulations for the conduct of collegiate competition have been developed by the National Joint Committee on Extramural Sports for College Women and are available from the committee for any specfic sport activity. While the statements of the National Joint Committee on Extramural Sports for College Women apply to approval for statewide or wider geographical tournaments, the principles may also be applicable to or guide the conduct of local and district tournaments.

In addition to the standards previously listed, other standards pertinent to the colleges are:

1. The amount and kind of intercollegiate competition should be determined by the women's physical education department.

2. The financial arrangements relative to all intercollegiate sport events should be administered with the approval of the women's physical education department.

3. The time involved in relation to intercollegiate competition should not interfere with the academic program of the institution sponsoring the event and should not make excessive demands upon the participants' academic schedules.

4. All housing arrangements relative to visiting participants should be approved by the women's physical education department.[2]

Girls' and women's athletics are occupying an increasingly more prominent role in the nation's schools and colleges. The programs appear to be well supervised, well controlled, and free of many of the abuses and problems associated with boys' and men's athletics. A large measure of the credit for developing such a sound program is due the DGWS.

_____

[2] Division for Girls and Women's Sports, "Statement of Policies for Competition in Girls and Women's Sports," *Journal of Health, Physical Education, and Recreation*, XXXIV (September 1963), 32.

CHAPTER VI

Athletic Standards
for Various Educational Levels

Elementary Schools

A discussion of the athletics program in the elementary school must be divided into two parts: the primary grades (1–3) and the intermediate grades (4–6).

Primary grades. Children in the primary grades generally range in age from five to eight years. They need a great deal of vigorous exercise to stimulate heart action and respiration and to build endurance. Opportunities for large-muscle development through active games and rhythm activities are necessary. Some organized group play, especially skipping and dancing games, will help develop a group feeling and will encourage the withdrawn child gradually to join the group.

The physical education program at this level should emphasize simple relays and games of loose organization. The games should have very few rules and should come to an early climax, for the attention span of the child at this age is not long.

The out-of-class program should be recreational in nature. The facilities and equipment at the school should be made available at specified hours for the students to participate informally in whatever activities they may choose.

Intermediate grades. The children in the intermediate grades range in age from eight to twelve years. Their need to develop strength and endurance is acute. They have learned to cooperate, and enjoy playing in groups; now they need organized games for team play. Their rhythmic sense is improved and they should be encouraged to engage in rhythmical activities, particularly folk- and square-dancing.

The physical education program at this level should emphasize the fundamental skills of climbing, throwing, catching, kicking, running, jumping, and tumbling, which are necessary for skillful per-

80

formance in athletics. Modified team games, relays, self-testing, and many movement experiences and activities should be emphasized.

Intramural competition may be initiated at this level. Opportunity to participate, rather than championships, should be emphasized. Schneider, in her report on physical education in the urban elementary schools, reports that 57 per cent of 523 school systems polled provide intramural sports programs beginning in Grades 2, 3, 4, 5, or 6.[1]

Basketball, softball, and touch football were the most popular sports among boys. By the end of the sixth grade, boys participate in intramural basketball (in 67 per cent of the school systems), softball (in 57 per cent), and football (in 50 per cent).[2] Girls competed in softball (in 37 per cent of the school systems), volleyball (in 27 per cent), and in basketball (in 25 per cent).[3] Volleyball was the most popular coeducational activity; boys and girls in 17 per cent of the school systems participate in it.[4]

There should be no varsity-type interscholastic athletics at the elementary school level. Competition sometimes involves sports days or play days, when teams from several schools assemble for a day of informal competition. Track and field days are especially popular. Emphasis is on participation and spectators are discouraged. Schneider reports that of the 523 school systems reporting, 58 per cent indicated that sports days are sponsored by the schools.[5] Although such a modified interscholastic program does exist in many schools, the authors recommend that athletic competition in the elementary school be limited to intramural programs.

Standards. The athletics program in the elementary school should stress what is good for the child and provide opportunities for a variety of experiences. All athletic activities should be geared to the developmental level of the individual child, and not just to his weight or chronological age. Children at this stage vary greatly in physical and psychological development, therefore an informal program which recognizes individual differences should be initiated.

---

[1] Elsa Schneider, *Physical Education in Urban Elementary Schools*, U.S. Department of Health, Education and Welfare, Bulletin No. 15 (Washington, D.C.: USGPO, 1959), p. 29.
[2] *Ibid.*
[3] *Ibid.*
[4] *Ibid.*
[5] *Ibid.*, p. 31.

The program should provide a wide variety of athletic experiences. Physical education activities should range from calisthenics through various athletic skills and games depending on the ability level of each child. There should not be undue concentration on developing skill in just a few sports; nor should children be pressured into conforming to adult standards of a rigid, highly organized, and highly competitive athletic program.

The Committee of School Health of the American Academy of Pediatrics reached the following conclusions and recommendations on competitive athletics for children twelve years of age and under:

1. All children should have opportunities to develop skill in a variety of activities.
2. All such activities should take into account the age and developmental level of the child.
3. (a) Athletic activities of elementary school children should be part of an over-all school program. Competent medical supervision of each child should be insured.
   (b) Health observation by teachers and others should be encouraged and help given by the physician.
4. Athletic activities outside the school program should be on an entirely voluntary basis without undue emphasis on any special program or sport, and without undue emphasis upon winning. These programs should also include competent medical supervision.
5. Competitive programs organized on school, neighborhood, and community levels will meet the needs of children twelve years of age and under. State, regional, and national tournaments; bowl, charity, and exhibition games are not recommended for this age group. Commercial exploitation in any form is unequivocally condemned.
6. Body-contact sports, particularly tackle football and boxing, are considered to have no place in programs for children of this age.
7. Competition is an inherent characteristic of growing, developing children. Properly guided, it is beneficial and not harmful to their development.
8. Schools and communities as a whole must be made aware of the needs for personnel, facilities, equipment, and supplies which will assure an adequate program for children in this age group.
9. All competitive athletic programs should be organized with the cooperation of interested medical groups who will insure adequate medical care before and during such programs. This should include thorough physical examinations at specified in-

tervals, teaching of health observation to teachers and coaches, as well as attention to factors such as injury, response to fatigue, individual emotional needs, and the risks of undue emotional strains.

10. Muscle testing is not, per se, a valid estimate of physical fitness, or of good health.

11. Participation in group activities is expected of every child. When there is a failure to [participate] . . . , or lack of interest, underlying physical or emotional causes should be sought.

12. Leadership for young children should be such that highly organized, highly competitive programs would be avoided. The primary consideration should be a diversity of wholesome childhood experiences which will aid in the proper physical and emotional development of the child into a secure and well-integrated adult.[6]

Junior High School

The purpose of the junior high school is to facilitate the transition from the elementary school to the high school. The nature of the junior high school curriculum is determined by the special growth pattern and developmental needs of the early adolescent. Consequently, the junior high school should not be modeled after the high school or the elementary school, but should develop as a separate and special type of school. The physical education program should reflect this philosophy; it should endeavor to provide activities geared to the developmental level of the students. The activities should be more advanced than the elementary school program and less complex than those in the high school program.

Characteristics of the junior high school student. Students in Grades 7–9 may be classified, biologically, as preadolescent to young adolescent. The preadolescent child has not yet had a growth spurt, whereas the young adolescent is passing through the rapid-growth period. The age range for junior high school students is normally eleven to fifteen years.

The junior high school student experiences a growth spurt which is brought on by internal physiological and biochemical changes. These changes become manifest by an increase in size and in the development of mature body contours and adult sexual character-

---

[6] Committee on School Health, American Academy of Pediatrics, "Competitive Athletics," *Pediatrics*, XVIII (October 1956), 675–76.

istics. The long bones of the arms and legs grow very rapidly in comparison to muscular development, resulting in a lack of fine motor control. This period is also characterized by the appearance of hair in the pubic area and in the armpits, and by the growth of sexual organs. Menstruation also begins during this period.

The growth spurt will occur at different times for different individuals. Each individual establishes his own growth pattern. Consequently, chronological grouping does not insure homogeneity, simply because some individuals of the same age will be at different levels of development.

Students in early adolescence, although possessing a great amount of energy, also have a tendency to become fatigued very easily. Therefore, it is important that they have opportunities for short periods of large-muscle activity which will result in a large expenditure of energy without bringing on fatigue.

The physiological changes which accompany early adolescence are responsible for psychological problems involving behavioral adjustment. This period is often characterized by mood fluctuations.

Many of the psychological strains are brought about by changes in group status. As the individual matures, he is faced with "critical adaptations . . . if he is to maintain status or find acceptance in the social groups with which he is identified or in which he desires membership."[7] Because the desire to belong to a group and to achieve popularity and recognition is strong in the young adolescent, he finds himself in a high-pressure environment which constantly challenges his ability to make adjustments and to adapt to changing situations.

Nature of the junior high school physical education program. In keeping with the nature of the junior high school educational program, the physical education program should seek to provide activities in a natural sequence or progression, based on the student's pattern of development. At the junior high school level, the program should provide experience in a wide variety of activities. The emphasis should be on improving fundamental athletic skills and on participating in competition in many different sports activities.

The Educational Policies Commission states that the athletic pro-

---

[7] H. E. Jones, "Principles and Methods of the Adolescent Growth Study," *Journal of Consulting Psychology*, III (September-October 1939), 157.

gram in the junior high school should be centered around "instruction in sports that takes place in the required classes in physical education. What is learned in such classes is applied in after-school and noon-hour games."[8] The Men's Division of Athletics of the American Association for Health, Physical Education, and Recreation recommends:

> ... the physical education program should provide opportunities for increased emphasis on instruction and practice in athletics, particularly in team games. The intense interest of adolescent boys in athletics together with their urgent desire to gain status among their peers, cause team games to be especially effective vehicles through which the desirable social development of the participants may be fostered.[9]

The instructional program in skills should be accompanied by an intramural program in all the activities included in the instructional program. The intramural program represents a laboratory experience in which the participant may compete for the sake of playing without undue emphasis on winning. Out of the intramural program, extramural activities may be developed in the form of sports days and play days with other schools in the neighborhood. In Norfolk, Virginia, citywide intramural tournaments have been held since 1950. Starting with only two sports, the program now encompasses nine sports and serves as the culmination of the individual schools' intramural programs.

Interscholastic athletics in the junior high school. The question of whether or not interscholastic athletics have a place in the junior high school is a highly controversial one. In 1958, Tompkins and Roe surveyed the principals of 2329 separately organized junior high schools, representing 90 per cent of the total junior high school enrollment in the United States. They found that about 85 per cent of those schools have some program of interscholastic athletics. Furthermore, they found that 78 per cent of the principals polled were in favor of interscholastic athletics at the junior high school level, 15.4 per cent were opposed, and 6.6 per cent did not indicate

---

[8] Educational Policies Commission, *School Athletics* (Washington, D.C.: National Education Association, 1954), p. 35.

[9] Men's Division of Athletics, American Association of Health, Physical Education, and Recreation, "Athletics in Education," *Journal of Health, Physical Education, and Recreation,* XXXIII (September 1962), 26.

a preference.[10] Those who approved interscholastic athletics felt that such activities were responsible for developing school spirit, that they provided wholesome competition, that they taught the values of sportsmanship and cooperation, that they emphasized desirable social standards of behavior, and that they served as an outlet for the release of the abundant energy of adolescence.[11] Reasons cited in opposition were that interscholastics tend to overexcite and overstrain physically and emotionally immature youngsters, that they require too much time and effort, that they are too expensive while involving only a few participants, that they are less effective than intramural programs, and that they place too great an emphasis on winning and are, therefore, too competitive.[12]

In contrast to the findings of Tompkins and Roe, many professional organizations had, prior to 1958, issued statements and resolutions indicating the dangers inherent in junior high school interscholastics and their opposition to them.

In 1938, the AAHPER published the following resolution pertaining to competition at the junior high school level.

> Inasmuch as pupils below the tenth grade are in the midst of the period of most rapid growth, with the consequent bodily weaknesses and maladjustments, partial ossification of bones, mental and emotional stresses, physiological readjustments, and the like, be it therefore resolved that the leaders in the field of physical and health education should do all in their power to discourage interscholastic competition at this age level because of its strenuous nature.[13]

In 1945, the American Medical Association recommended:

> Interschool athletic leagues should be confined to the senior high schools and should be financed by school funds and administered by school officers. Interschool activities for junior high school pupils should be limited to occasional invitational meets or games. Junior high school boys should not compete in football.[14]

---

[10] Ellsworth Tompkins and Virginia Roe, "A Survey of Interscholastic Athletic Programs in Separately Organized Junior High Schools," *The Bulletin of the National Association of Secondary School Principals,* XLII: 241 (November 1958), 3.

[11] *Ibid.,* p. 30.

[12] *Ibid.,* p. 31.

[13] American Association of Health, Physical Education, and Recreation, "Two Important Resolutions," *Journal of Health, Physical Education, and Recreation,* IX (October 1938), 48.

[14] American Medical Association, *Suggested School Health Policies,* 3rd ed. (Chicago: American Medical Association, 1956), pp. 27–28.

In 1951, the American Association of School Administrators stated:

> Interscholastic athletics are not recommended for junior high school boys. At these levels most boys are prepubescent, growing rapidly, and insufficiently developed to withstand the physical and emotional strain of interscholastic competition.[15]

In 1952, the Joint Committee on Athletic Competition for Children of Elementary and Junior High School Age, recommended:

> No interschool competition of a varsity pattern. Interschool competition of a varsity pattern and similarly organized competition under auspices of other community agencies are definitely disapproved for children below the ninth grade.[16]

In 1954, the Educational Policies Commission recommended:

> No junior high school should have a "school team" that competes with school teams of other junior high schools in organized leagues or tournaments. Varsity-type interscholastics for junior high school boys and girls should not be permitted.[17]

It is obvious that the findings of Tompkins and Roe and the efforts of professional organizations to restrain interscholastic competition at the junior high school level are highly contradictory. Since 1958, the junior high school interscholastic program has continued and widespread opposition has persisted. The resolution of this controversial issue depends on an appreciation of the pertinent physiological and psychological factors.

That the physiological factors of participation in interschool athletics at the junior high school level should be considered first is indicative of their importance in resolving this issue. The growth-spurt characteristic of the early adolescent is responsible for many of these physiological considerations. Because muscular development fails to keep pace with long-bone growth, joints and bones are not fully protected. The child is, therefore, extremely susceptible to

---

[15] American Association of School Administrators, *Health in Schools,* Twentieth Yearbook, (Washington, D.C.: American Association of School Administrators, 1951), p. 197.

[16] Joint Committee on Athletic Competition for Elementary and Junior High School Age Children, *Desirable Athletic Competition for Children* (Washington, D.C.: American Association for Health, Physical Education, and Recreation, 1952), p. 4.

[17] Educational Policies Commission, *op. cit.,* p. 36.

joint dislocations and bone injuries, especially to the epiphyseal cartilages, which are not yet calcified.[18,19]

The report of the opinions of 220 medical specialists (including seventy-eight pediatricians, thirty-three cardiologists, forty-three orthopedic surgeons, twenty-one physiologists, and forty-five general practitioners), concerning the factors which they deemed valid in determining the type and extent of athletic activity for children ages twelve to fifteen, indicated that 45 per cent considered the factor of greater vulnerability of joints to injury important. Furthermore, 47 per cent indicated there was a special hazard in connection with the fracture of the epiphyseal area of the long bones.[20]

However, there is no conclusive evidence that boys are injured more often or more seriously in well-organized junior high school interschool athletic programs than in high school interscholastics.

Hibbert reported that, in football, a junior high school boy has a 500 per cent greater chance of being injured than a senior high school participant.[21] In Iowa, a study reported the incidence of athletic injury in senior high school was 189.1 injuries per thousand students as compared with 46.4 injuries for every thousand junior school students.[22] Krogman, in a study of football, estimated that one in every four boys suffers some type of injury, and that one third of those injured sustain more critical injuries, such as fractures, concussions, and internal injuries.[23] Burnett reports that sandlot or unorganized football games cause the most critical and the highest number of injuries.[24] It may only be concluded that, to avoid severity and frequency of injury, some type of organized program of competition is indicated.

In skill development, the child develops certain sets of muscles more than others. In general, strenuous athletics tend to develop the

---

[18] John L. Reichert, "Competitive Athletics for Pre-Teen-Age Children," *Journal of the American Medical Association*, CLXVI (April 5, 1958), 1703.

[19] Committee on School Health, American Academy of Pediatrics, *op. cit.*

[20] Joint Committee on Athletic Competition for Children of Elementary and Junior High School Age, *op. cit.*, p. 9.

[21] Russell W. Hibbert, Jr., "High School Football Injuries," *Rocky Mountain Medical Journal*, XLVII (April 1950), 276–77.

[22] Iowa High School Insurance Company, *Report* (Des Moines, January 1, 1959).

[23] Wilton Marion Krogman, "Child Growth and Football," *Journal of Health, Physical Education, and Recreation*, XXVI (September 1958), 12.

[24] Joseph H. Burnett, "Football—A Review of Injuries in Boston Secondary Schools," *New England Journal of Medicine*, CCXIII (September 26, 1940), 488.

flexor muscles more than the extensor muscles. The resultant shift in stress affects the development of the bones to which the muscles attach. According to Wolff's law, changes in the internal structure and external appearance of the bones are determined by the application of such stress. This may lead to poor posture, resulting in a skeletally malaligned individual.[25]

Growth is an energy-consuming process. Krogman estimates that only 10 to 20 per cent of all available energy in the early adolescent may be channeled into activity; the remaining 80 to 90 per cent is required for growth processes.[26] Hein reports that reasonable activity will stimulate and assist the growth process, but that unnecessary emotional or physical stress may have the opposite effect. Such a child may enter a fatigue cycle characterized by fatigue leading to impaired nutrition, impaired general health, and inability to rest properly leading to greater fatigue.[27] Normally, when a child is tired, he will stop playing in order to rest. The danger arises from the high emotional and social pressures of the formal organized program of competition in which the individual is encouraged to exceed his endurance limits. Of the 220 medical specialists, 61 per cent felt there was more likelihood for activity to be carried past the stages of healthful fatigue to harmful exhaustion in interscholastics at the junior high school level.[28]

In regard to growth and athletics, the literature reveals two major points: those who participate in athletics at the junior high school level are selected for superiority in body size, but there is inconclusive evidence concerning the effects of athletics on growth. Clarke and Petersen report that boys making the teams in interschool athletics at the junior high school level are definitely superior in maturity, body size, muscular strength and explosive muscular power.[29] Shuck, in a study to evaluate growth and development in terms of body shape, body size, and speed of growth in 366 junior high school boys, concluded that athletes were larger in body size than

---

[25] Reichert, *loc. cit.*

[26] Krogman, *op. cit.*, p. 78.

[27] Fred V. Hein, "Educational Aspects of Athletics for Children," *Journal of the American Medical Association*, CLXVIII (November 15, 1958), 1434–38.

[28] Joint Committee on Athletic Competition for Elementary and Junior High School Age Children, *loc. cit.*

[29] H. Harrison Clarke and Kay H. Petersen, "Contrast of Maturational, Structural, and Strength Characteristics of Athletes and Nonathletes ten to fifteen Years of Age," *Research Quarterly*, XXXII (May 1961), 175.

nonathletes. His study indicated that athletes were selected for superiority in body size and speed of growth as well as for skill.[30]

Rowe, in a study comparing the growth experienced by a group of athletes to that experienced by nonathletes, found that athletes did not grow as much as nonathletes.[31] One obvious explanation is that the athletes have already experienced their growth spurt, whereas the nonathlete has not. McGraw found that athletic participation stimulated growth.[32] Shuck, in his study of the effects of athletic competition on growth and development in junior high school boys, concluded that there was no pronounced retardation or acceleration in growth and development among athletes resulting from athletic participation.[33]

A few studies show that some junior high school boys who participate in athletics are those who possess the greatest amount of physiological maturity. This might explain why these athletes show less growth as a result of athletic competition. In such cases the factors of bone growth, muscular imbalance, and fatigue would not be so critical for them since they have, for the most part, passed through the growth spurt. Therefore, only the physiologically mature should be permitted to participate in interscholastic athletics at the junior high level. Lowman found that 85 per cent of a group of several hundred orthopedists, replying to a survey, indicated that athletic competition should only be for the physiologically mature.[34]

Thus, the need arises for a method of measuring physiological maturity. Several techniques or criteria have been employed in the past, such as beard growth, urinanalysis, measurement of height and size, and pubic hair development. It is generally agreed, however,

---

[30] Gilbert R. Shuck, "Effects of Athletic Competition of the Growth and Development of Junior High School Boys," *Research Quarterly,* XXXIII (May 1962), 290.

[31] Floyd A. Rowe, "Growth Comparisons of Athletes and Nonathletes," *Research Quarterly,* IV (October 1933), 115.

[32] L. W. McGraw, "Comparison of Physical Growth and Development of Athletes and Non-Athletes at the Junior High School Level," *Report to Research Section, American Association of Health, Physical Education, and Recreation,* National Convention, Chicago, March 1956. Cited in Creighton J. Hale, "Athletics for Pre-High School Age Children," *Journal of Health, Physical Education, and Recreation,* XXX (December 1959), 19.

[33] Shuck, *loc. cit.*

[34] C. L. Lowman, "The Vulnerable Age," *Journal of Health, Physical Education, and Recreation,* XVIII (November 1947), 635.

that the single most dependable criterion of maturity is the evalua-
tion of bone development by X ray.[35] It is questionable whether this
practice is widely used in junior high school interscholastic athletics
because of the time involved and the cost of skeletal X rays. Certainly, with the dangers of injury and fatigue inherent during the
growth spurt, all participants in interscholastic athletics should be
classified according to physiological maturity by X ray assessment,
and only those already physiologically mature should be permitted
to play.

The junior high school student looks to peer-group membership
for status, prestige, and recognition. These groups place a high value
on physical ability. Therefore, it has been argued that interschool
athletics at the junior high school level contribute to a student's se-
curity and social adjustment.[36] McGraw and Tolbert concluded that
junior high school boys achieve more popularity through participation in interscholastic sports than in any other way.[37] Mussen and
Jones compared eighteen late-maturing and sixteen early-maturing
adolescent boys. Their results showed that a high aggressive drive
and an intense drive for social acceptance are more characteristic of
the physically retarded than of the physically accelerated. In general,
their data support the findings of earlier studies which showed that
the high social drives common to late-maturing adolescents stem
from feelings of insecurity, rejection, and inadequacy. The adverse
effects of such drives are manifest in childish, affected, attention-
getting techniques.[38] The point is that the early-maturing adolescents
make the junior high school interscholastic teams. These boys receive the prestige which their peer groups attach to athletics at this
age level. This serves to heighten and dramatize the effects of athletics on the late-maturing adolescent who does not play interscholastics because he cannot make the team. Interscholastic athletics,
therefore, only increase the adverse effects on the personality of the
late-maturers described by Mussen and Jones.

Regarding social adjustment, Salz, in a study utilizing five person-

[35] Krogman, *op. cit.,* pp. 77–78.

[36] Ray Duncan, "Scope of Interscholastic Athletics," *Bulletin of the National Association of Secondary School Principals,* XLIV (May 1960), 87.

[37] L. W. McGraw and J. W. Tolbert, "Sociometric Status and Athletic Ability Junior High School Boys," *Research Quarterly,* XXIV (March 1953), 72.

[38] Paul Henry Mussen and Mary C. Jones, "The Behavior-Inferred Motivations of Late- and Early-Maturing Boys," *Child Development,* XXIX (1958), 67.

ality tests, found that those boys who had been exposed to varying levels of competition scored significantly higher on the personality tests than boys who did not have competitive athletic experiences.[39] Biddulph compared the personal and social adjustment of high school boys of high athletic achievement to that of boys of low athletic achievement. He found those ranking high in achievement demonstrated a significantly greater degree of personal and social adjustment.[40]

Proponents of interscholastic athletics for junior high school boys argue that participation contributes to emotional control.[41] Those opposed are concerned that high-pressure competition may lead to strong emotional reaction in youngsters, adversely affecting their emotional development.[42] The controversy lies, therefore, in the level of intensity of competition which will contribute to emotional development. Maksim and Landis reflect this feeling in their report on the emotional aspects of athletics. They concluded that the emotional development of children twelve years old and under benefits from opportunities and encouragement to participate in athletics. Activities, properly selected, taking into consideration individual differences in levels of physical and mental development, will enhance both emotional and physical growth.[43] It is important, therefore, to avoid any high-pressure elements which might lead to unhealthy emotional development. The Joint Committee on Athletic Competition for Children of Elementary and Junior High School Age has identified the following undesirable high-pressure elements:

> Highly organized competition in the form of leagues or championships. Overemphasis by means of newspapers, radio, television, or similar media. Stress on individuals rather than teams, such as selection of "all-star" teams.

---

[39] Art Salz, "Comparative Study of Personalities of Little League Champions, Other Players in Little League, and Nonplaying Peers." Unpublished master's thesis presented at Pennsylvania State University, University Park, Pennsylvania, 1957. Cited in Hale, *op. cit.*, p. 20.

[40] Lowell G. Biddulph, "Athletic Achievement and the Personal Social Adjustment of High School Boys," *Research Quarterly*, XXV (March 1955), 1.

[41] Louis E. Alley, "Interscholastic Athletics for Junior High School Boys," *Bulletin of the National Association of Secondary School Principals*, XLIV (May, 1960), 98.

[42] *Ibid.*, p. 97.

[43] George Maksim and Paul E. Landis, "Emotional Aspects of Athletics for Children and Youth," *Report of the Fifth National Conference on Physicians and Schools*, Bureau of Health Education, American Medical Association, October 1955, p. 18.

Tournaments, frequent contests, long seasons, "little" bowl games, or other procedures that cause pressures or that may make undue physical demands on young boys or girls.

Games or contests played at night or at other times, outside usual school or recreation hours.

Travel beyond the immediate neighborhood (or in the case of small rural schools, a nearby community).

Encouragement of partisan spectators and supporters—any pressures that come from the social situation that place undue value on an informal game.

"Grooming" of players for a high school or college team, proselyting or inducements of any kind to cause a good player to leave his normal group and play with another team.

Commercial promotions which, under various guises, seek to exploit youth for selfish purposes.

Competitions in which a selected few players are given a large and disproportionate share of facilities and of the time and attention of staff members, with the resultant neglect of a large number of children.[44]

Conclusions and standards. It would seem apparent, from the discussion above, that there are both physiological and psychological advantages and disadvantages for the junior high school participant in competitive athletics. It would also seem apparent that it is possible to reap the benefits of competition without incurring its disadvantages, in a program that excludes interscholastic athletics at the junior high school level. The following statement of standards was developed by the Subcommittee on Junior High School Athletics of the Joint Committee on Standards in Athletics. This statement has been endorsed by the American Association for Health, Physical Education, and Recreation; the National Association of Secondary School Principals; and the Society of the State Directors of Health, Physical Education, and Recreation.

In developing a program of athletic activities, the *first* duty of a junior high school is to provide opportunities for *all* students to participate. Because of limitations in space, facilities, equipment, and adequately trained personnel, these opportunities can best be provided in most junior high schools through:

1. *The required program of physical education:* A daily period of physical education for all students in which instruction and guided practice are provided in a variety of physical activities that are suited to the nature and needs of the junior high school student.

---

[44] Joint Committee on Athletic Competition for Children of Elementary and Junior High School Age, *op. cit.,* p. 405.

2. *The intramural program:* A well-organized and well-conducted program of intramural (within the school) competition in which opportunities are provided for *all* students to put into practice the knowledge and skills acquired in the required physical education program.

3. *The physical recreation program:* A program in which *all* students are provided opportunities to participate *informally* in a variety of vigorous activities.

In those junior high schools in which adequate programs of required physical education, intramurals, and physical recreation are provided for all students, a limited program of interscholastic athletics provides for boys with superior athletic ability additional opportunities to fully develop and utilize this talent. Such programs of interscholastic athletics should be organized and conducted in accordance with the principles outlined below.

1. The interscholastic athletics program for boys in the junior high school should make definite contributions toward the accomplishment of the educational objectives of the school.

2. The interscholastic athletics program for boys in the junior high school should supplement rather than serve as a substitute for adequate programs of required physical education, intramurals, and physical recreation for all students.

3. The interscholastic athletic program for boys in the junior high school should, under the administration and supervision of the appropriate school officials, be conducted by men with adequate professional preparation in physical education.

4. The interscholastic athletics program for boys in the junior high school should be so conducted that the physical welfare of the participants is protected and fostered.[45]

High School and College or University

The athletics program in high schools and colleges will be very similar in appearance, although the college or university program may be much wider in scope. The basis, as in all programs, is the required service program. Most high schools require participation in physical education classes each year. Most colleges have a minimum two-year physical education requirement. Highest standards

[45] Louis E. Alley, "Standards for Junior High School Athletics," *Administration of High School Athletics, Report of the First National Conference on Secondary School Athletic Administration* (Washington, D.C.: American Association for Health, Physical Education, and Recreation, 1963), p. 19. Also available under the title *Standards for Junior High School Athletics* (Washington, D.C.: American Association for Health, Physical Education, and Recreation, 1963).

require that all students in the high school have a daily physical education class. In the colleges, a required program for all students through the sophomore year is a minimum requirement.

The athletics program begins with the intramural program. This program should endeavor to include as many participants as is possible. It should include all activities which are regularly included in the required physical education program plus any other suitable activities. In addition, many schools schedule extramural competition with other nearby schools and colleges.

Interscholastic and intercollegiate competition should be carried on within a formal structure of well-defined policies consistent with the philosophy and objectives of the institution.

Standards. The following basic principles apply to both interscholastic and intercollegiate athletics. The interscholastic and intercollegiate athletic program should:

1. Be an integral part of the general educational program;
2. Complement and supplement the total physical education program;
3. Be controlled in the same manner as the general education program;
4. Be conducted by qualified phyiscal educators;
5. Be conducted in a manner that will enhance the health of the participants;
6. Be conducted according to the rules and regulations and recommendations of professional associations, leagues, and athletic conferences.[46]

The "cardinal athletic principles" of the Joint Committee on Athletic Problems in Education of the American Association for Health, Physical Education, and the National Federation of State High School Athletic Associations, are particularly valuable to educators and are an indication of guides that are needed for policy formulation for the conduct of the interscholastic athletics program:

> Schools provide opportunity for each individual to develop himself to the limit of his capacity in the skills, appreciations, and health concepts which engender personal satisfaction and civic usefulness. A good school program includes the means for exploring many fields of activity. One such field is that which involves athletic performance. Participation in and appreciation of the skills in a sports contest is a part of enjoyable living. Ability to recognize degrees of proficiency in these skills is one important attribute of the well-balanced individual. The perfectly timed and coordinated activities by which an individual, or a team, strives to achieve a definite objec-

---

[46] Men's Division of Athletics, *op. cit.,* p. 27.

tive is an exemplification of coordination and efficiency. A good school program provides a mixture of benevolent restrictions and freedom, of mental growth and physical development, of liberties and restraints. Developing and maintaining a physically fit nation is one of its important aims.

For developing endurance, strength, alertness, and coordination, contests and conditioning exercises have been made a part of the school program. Nature wisely insured a degree of physical development and social adjustment by endowing the individual with a desire to play. Around this desire, as a nucleus, can be built a complete program of beneficial exercises in which healthful and satisfying habits and attitudes are stressed.

To be of maximum effectiveness, the athletic program will:

1. Be closely coordinated with the general instructional program and properly articulated with the other departments of the school;

2. Be such that the number of students accommodated and the educational aims achieved justify the use of tax funds for its support and also warrant the use of other sources of income;

3. Justify the time and attention which is given to the collection of such funds which will not interfere with the efficiency of the athletic program or of any other department of the school;

4. Confine the school athletic activity to events which are sponsored and supervised by the proper school authorities so that any exploitation or improper use of prestige built up by school teams or members of such teams may be avoided;

5. Be planned in such a way as to result in opportunity for many individuals to explore a wide variety of sports and to set reasonable season limits for each listed sport;

6. Be controlled in such a way as to avoid the elements of professionalism and commercialism which tend to grow up in connection with widely publicized "bowl" contests, barnstorming trips, and interstate or intersectional contests which require excessive travel expense or loss of school time or which are claimed to be justified by educational travel values;

7. Be kept free from the type of contest which involves a gathering of so-called all-stars from different schools to participate in contests which may be used as a gathering place for representatives of certain colleges or professional organizations who are interested in soliciting athletic talent for their teams;

8. Include educative exercises to reach all nonparticipating students and community followers of the school teams in order to insure a proper understanding and appreciation of the sports skills and of the need for adherence to principles of game ethics;

9. Encourage a balanced program of intramural activity in grades below the ninth to make it unnecessary to sponsor contests of a championship nature in these grades;

10. Engender respect for the rules and policies under which the school conducts its program.[47]

In 1951, the Joint Committee on Standards for Interscholastic Athletics of the National Association of Secondary School Principals, the National Federation of State High School Associations, and the American Association for Health, Physical Education, and Recreation, made specific recommendations for the implementation of the Cardinal Athletic Principles. A selective sampling of these recommendations is presented here:

1. The program of athletics should be developed in light of desirable standards of health and safety:

(a) A health examination should be required prior to participation.

(b) A physician should be present at all contests where there is danger of injury.

(c) The written recommendation of a physician is required before an ill or injured player is permitted to return to the game.

(d) The coach or faculty member in charge and, if possible, all players should be well versed in first aid procedures and in training procedures.

(e) Players incurring injuries of the head, spine, or neck should be removed from play immediately and examined by a physician.

(f) There should be a written policy in every school regarding the responsibility for and the procedure to be followed when injuries are incurred in athletics.

(g) Only the best protective equipment that can be purchased should be utilized, and players should be properly fitted.

(h) Competition should take place only between teams of comparable ability, and playing seasons should be of reasonable duration.

(i) At least two weeks of physical conditioning should be given prior to any games being held.

(j) Playing surfaces should be constructed and maintained according to the highest safety standards. Equipment and facilities should meet same standards.

2. Good citizenship should be an objective of all coaching in interschool competition.

(a) Many values exist in athletics besides winning.

(b) Athletics must contribute to the development of such traits as truthfulness, fair play, honesty, courtesy, self-discipline, courage, self-restraint, and loyalty.

3. The Cardinal Athletic Principles express desirable athletic policies and therefore should be publicized as much as possible.

---

[47] Joint Committee on Athletic Problems in Education, "Cardinal Athletic Principles," *Journal of Health, Physical Education, and Recreation,* XVIII (September 1947), 435, 557–58.

4. Schools should exercise caution in athletics and particularly in contact sports to see that competition has been properly equated. For example, participants of normal high school age should not participate against players below normal high school age where size and other aspects of maturity show a wide disparity.

(a) Players mature at different rates of speed and therefore this is an important factor to consider when properly equating players for competitive athletics.

(b) High school students should not compete with members of a college of university, a preparatory school, or other institution which include postgraduates, or against independent teams sponsored by an "outside" organization.

(c) School authorities in charge of athletics should be legally certified teaching, supervisory, and administrative personnel directly under the superintendent of schools.

5. Eligibility requirements should be strictly adhered to.

6. Solicitation of athletes through such means as tryouts or competitive bidding by colleges and universities is strongly opposed.

7. National high school championship contests in any sport are forbidden.[48]

In 1952, the North Central Association of Colleges and Secondary Schools published a revised athletic policy that was clear, concise, and far-reaching in its impact. This document, excerpts of which are included below in adapted form, is typical of the standards which must prevail in an intercollegiate program based on sound educational objectives.[49]

1. *Athletic Purposes:* the purposes of the athletic program of an institution should be clearly stated in printed form. Purposes should be determined by the faculty, should appear in the catalog, and should make clear the official position of the institution pertaining to athletics as they relate to the educational program as a whole.

2. *Administration:* the chief administrative officer of a college or university is responsible for the intercollegiate athletics in his institution. Although the faculty will exercise the same powers in athletics it possesses in other areas of the institution's educational program, the chief administrative officer must assume the role of leader.

3. *Staff:* the coaching staff should be composed of regular members of the faculty and possess the necessary qualifications which such posi-

---

48 Joint Committee on Standards for Interscholastic Athletics, "Standards in Athletics for Boys in Secondary Schools," *Journal of Health, Physical Education, and Recreation,* XXII (September 1951), 16.

49 Commission on Colleges and Universities, *An Interpretation of the Revised Policy on Intercollegiate Athletics of the North Central Association* (Chicago: North Central Association of Colleges and Secondary Schools, 1952), pp. 9–15.

tions imply. The coaching staff should also enjoy all the privileges that other members of the faculty enjoy.

4. *Recruitment of Athletes:* players should be bona fide students in the educational program. The recruitment of students of athletic prowess for the purpose of developing winning athletic teams is unworthy of an institution of higher education.

5. *Admissions:* the regular admissions officer and/or committee should act upon all applications for admissions regardless of whether or not the applicant is an athlete.

6. *Subsidization:* the subsidization of athletes as athletes is disapproved. The contribution a student can make to the winning of athletic contests should not be taken into consideration at all in the granting of financial aid of any kind.

7. *Academic Requirements:* athletes should meet the same academic requirements expected of other students.

8. *Health:* the health of students who are athletes should not be exploited for the benefit of the institution or the public.

9. *Finances:* all activities of the institution of higher learning should have the same financial control policies—athletics should not be an exception.

10. *Sportsmanship:* any athlete representing a college or university should display the highest standards of sportsmanship in order to bring credit to that institution.

11. *Cooperation with Athletic Organizations:* institutions devoted to good sportsmanship will work closely with such organizations as the National Collegiate Athletic Association, the American Council of Education, and the various athletic conferences, in an attempt to establish high standards for intercollegiate athletics.

12. *Relations with Secondary Schools:* the athletic policies of any institution of higher learning should help and never deter secondary schools in their desire to maintain sound standards in athletics. The recommendations of such organizations as the National Association of Secondary School Principals and the National Federation of State Athletic Associations should be followed in this regard.

Summary of Selected Recommended Standards for Varsity Interscholastic and Intercollegiate Athletics

1. Organization
   (a) The wholesome conduct of the athletic program should be the ultimate responsibility of the school administration.
   (b) Athletic policy should be adopted, evaluated, and supervised by a faculty committee.
   (c) Athletic policy should be implemented by the director of physical education and the director of athletics.

    (d) Athletics should be organized as an integral part of the department of physical education.

2. Staff
    (a) All members of the coaching staff should be members of the faculty.
    (b) All coaches should be hired on their qualifications to assume educational responsibilities, and not on their ability to produce winning teams.
    (c) All coaches should enjoy the same privileges of tenure, rank, and salary which are accorded other similarly qualified faculty members.
    (d) All public school coaches should be certified in physical education.

3. Finances
    (a) The financing of interscholastic and intercollegiate athletics should be governed by the same policies that control the financing of all other educational activities within an institution.
    (b) Gate receipts should be considered an incidental source of revenue.

4. Health and safety
    (a) An annual physical examination should be required of all participants; a physical examination on a seasonal basis would be preferable.
    (b) Each school should have a written policy for the implementation of an injury-care program.
    (c) Each school should have a written policy concerning the responsibility for athletic injuries and should provide or make available athletic accident insurance.
    (d) All coaches should be well qualified in the care and prevention of athletic injuries.
    (e) A doctor should be present at all contests at which injury is possible.
    (f) Only that equipment offering the best protection should be purchased.
    (g) Proper fitting of all protective equipment should be insured.
    (h) Competition should be scheduled only between teams of comparable ability.
    (i) Games should not be played until players have had a minimum of three weeks of physical conditioning and drill.
    (j) Playing fields should meet standards for size and safety.

5. Eligibility
    (a) All schools should honor and respect the eligibity rules and regulations of respective local, state, and national athletic associations.
    (b) A student who is not making normal progress toward a degree or diploma should not be allowed to participate.

6. Recruiting
   (a) The athletic teams of each school should be composed of bona fide students who live in the school district or who were attracted to the institution by its educational program.
   (b) All candidates for admission to a school should be evaluated according to the same high standards.
   (c) All financial aid should be administered with regard to need and according to the same standards for all students. The recipient of financial aid should be given a statement of the amount, duration, and conditions of the award.
7. Awards
   (a) The value of athletic awards should be limited.
   (b) There should be no discrimination between awards for different varsity sports.
   (c) The presentation of all-star, most-valuable-player, and most-improved-player awards should be discouraged.

CHAPTER VII

International Implications of Competitive Athletics in America

The international implications of athletics are well illustrated by the following anecdote told by Jesse Owens, concerning an experience he had in the 1936 Olympic games:

> I met a broad jumper named Lutz Long, whom I had never heard of before. We had a "book" on every boy in the world who was jumping twenty-four to twenty-five feet or better, and his name was not on the list. I was having trouble trying to qualify—I had fouled once, didn't jump far enough on the second jump, and had to move the take-off board back. Lutz Long held the tape line for me and laid my sweat shirt on the line near the take-off board. I came down the runway and qualified. We got into the finals and it was a seesaw battle for six jumps. I won the Olympic title on the second to the last jump. At the last jump, with the pressure off, I was able to set the Olympic record, which held until 1960.
>
> But that is not the important thing. When we had stepped off the victory stand, I was stopped by a newspaperman. Lutz Long had picked up his sweat shirt and was on his way to the dressing room; I took several quick steps and caught up with him. As we walked around the track trying to communicate, each in his own language, unconsciously he placed his arm on my shoulder, and I unconsciously placed my arm around his waist and we walked in this manner; 120,000 people stood and cheered that day until we had walked to the shadows of the dressing room.
>
> And then began letters of friendship across the ocean. In 1938 I got my last letter from Lutz Long, because Hitler had invaded Poland. In 1951 when I was sitting in a hotel in Hamburg, Germany, a woman and a boy entered the lobby. The moment I laid eyes upon the lad I knew that he was the son of Lutz Long. Under his arm he had a book, and in it were some of the letters that I had written to his father and pictures of his dad and me. Then began a friendship between the son and myself. In 1960 he was at the Olympic games in Rome as a representative of Western Germany. He is now corresponding with the boy from Boston who won in 1960, in the same way that I corresponded with his father. Sports

are indeed a universal language, helping to build an understanding of mankind.[1]

Jesse Owens' experiences are by no means unique. Countless hundreds of individuals have shared similar experiences with athletes from other countries. Sports are, indeed, a universal language. In the recent quest for world unity, of which the United Nations is an obvious example, it was apparent that it would be necessary to bridge the gaps set by the multitude of linguistic, religious, and ethnic differences which exist in the world. It has become clear, in recent years, that these gaps are best bridged by experiences which are common to all people. Such things as art, music, drama, literature, and play are natural and spontaneous responses to the needs and desires of all men. All these activities provide opportunities for repeated contact between individuals, thereby broadening the channels of personal communication between Americans and persons of other countries. Better communication lends to better understanding. Therefore, athletics represent just one of many bridges to mutual understanding.

Examples of Athletics on
the International Level

There are many examples of athletics on an international level. By far the most well-known are the Olympic games. The Olympics began in ancient Greece in 776 B.C. and were held every four years until they were abolished in A.D. 294 by the Roman Emperor Theodosius. They probably originated as festivals of various kinds in which athletics played a major part. The Olympic games included foot races over various distances, armor races, boxing, chariot races, and a pentathlon. The individual winners became public heroes in the eyes of the Greeks. As the years went by, the material rewards of victory in the Olympic games in the form of gifts, tax exemptions, and other favors, led to unsportsmanlike practices. By the time the Romans had conquered Greece, the Olympic Games had become exhibitions of professionalism and brutality. This trend led to their abolition by Theodosius.

---

[1] Jesse Owens, "What Athletics Mean to Me," in *Values in Sports, Report of a Joint National Conference of the Division for Girls' and Women's Sports and the Division of Men's Athletics* (Washington, D.C.: American Association for Health, Physical Education, and Recreation, 1963), pp. 85–86.

The modern Olympic Games were revived by Baron Pierre de Coubertin in 1896. While studying the mushrooming sports movements in America and England, de Coubertin recognized the potential value of international competition. He was able to organize an International Olympic Committee in 1894, which approved Athens as the site of the first modern Olympic Games in 1896. Since then, the Olympics have been held every four years, except during the period of World War II. Women entered competition in 1912, and the winter sports were added in 1934. The Olympics were conceived to honor individual winners rather than countries. No nation is officially declared the winner, although the newspapers have devised a point system by which unofficial standings of the various teams are maintained.

In addition to the Olympics, there are many other international competitions, conferences, and clinics. The People-to-People Sports Committee, organized as a part of the People-to-People program of the Eisenhower administration and since incorporated as a separate citizens' movement, has sent many high school and college athletes, teams, and coaches abroad. In addition, they have sponsored tours of the United States by many foreign teams. The Pan-American Games and the United States-Russian track-meet series are other significant examples. Many prominent coaches and physical educators have participated in programs initiated by the State Department of the federal government to consult and, in many cases, to train athletic teams in other countries. The exchange of students and teachers under the Fulbright Act has been very significant in establishing good international relations. Almost all the various physical education associations—the American Association for Health, Physical Education, and Recreation, the American Academy of Physical Education, and the National Association of Physical Education for College Women—sponsor programs in international athletics. The newly organized International Council on Health, Physical Education, and Recreation and the United Nations Educational, Scientific, and Cultural Organization are both concerned with international cooperation in education leading to international understanding.

Values

The values of any program which brings together the people of the world in close personal contact cannot be overemphasized. That the dynamic aspects of athletics provide many opportunities for such contact is undeniable. The contributions of athletics to improving international relations should be exploited to the fullest possible extent. A first requisite of world peace is world understanding.

International competition and the exchange of coaches and teachers, effective as they are, reach only a limited number of well-skilled athletes. Much can be done here in America in our athletics programs to further international cooperation and understanding. Sports days or play days can be organized around an international theme in which games of other countries are played. International concepts may be developed through the use of costumes, music, and the presence of individuals from other lands.

In 1961, McDermott reported that the Sports Club of Irvington Elementary School (Irvington, New York) had been successful in developing international understanding.[2] The Sports Club was designed to study games and sports of all kinds. Since the elementary school physical education program provided the student with a good background in various American games and sports, they decided to study children's games of foreign countries. Each member wrote to a foreign embassy of his choice for information about games played in that country. As answers were received, those games were played which equipment and facilities allowed. Whenever a sport (such as skiing, jai alai, or skin-diving) could not be played, movies of the sport were shown.

The discussions which followed highlighted many similarities between countries. Many children were surprised to learn that children of other countries play games similar to those in America, and that, in many cases, the American game is derived from the game of another country. The children realized that despite nationality, race, customs, traditions, or religious beliefs, children all over the world like to play games and engage in sports. The knowledge that children of other lands play outdoors more than American children do

---

[2] Edward J. McDermott, "International Understanding Through Sports," *New York State Education*, XLVIII (April 1961), 22f.

led one child to surmise that the other countries were not as rich as ours and could not afford to build gymnasiums.

Wherever possible, the program of the Sports Club was integrated into the school curriculum. Each student was required to rewrite his letter until the grammar and spelling were correct and the letter was neat and legible. As answers were received, students were paired in teams to explain and teach each game. All the materials that were received were placed in the school library as reference material.

One sixth-grade child summed up the experience when he said that they not only had fun playing the games but they learned many things about other countries as well. In conclusion, McDermott states:

> ... we are accomplishing in the Irvington Sports Club, to a small degree, the same objectives that the country as a whole is trying to achieve by sending and receiving exchange students from abroad and by the exchange with various countries of cultural, scientific, athletic and agricultural missions.[3]

Conclusion

Sports are not confined to the United States; they are international in scope. People the world over are interested in athletics, games, and other physical education activities. A tennis match at Forest Hills or Wimbledon will attract players from Australia, Brazil, Mexico, the Philippines, Great Britain, and France. A college track team will travel across the waters to display its skill in a foreign country. The British Open Golf Tournament attracts enthusiasts from all over the world. The Russian basketball team may travel to the United States and play in several contests with American teams from coast to coast. Skaters and other participants in winter sports from different countries display their prowess at Saint Moritz. The Olympic festival is, of course, the greatest and most famous sports gathering, bringing together athletes from many nations. Through these international events, sports have potentialities for promoting international understanding, through which people of many countries may be brought closer together.

Through sports competition in such games as tennis, golf, crew,

---

[3] *Ibid.*, p. 23.

polo, soccer, and hockey; sports medicine conferences where research methods and studies are exchanged on everything from training techniques to new equipment; hospitality to foreign students and athletes; good working relationships among educational institutions; good will is promoted and the people of many cultures come to a fuller understanding of one another. The emphasis in all of these activities should be on friendly competition, sociability, and the desire to meet the needs of people everywhere. The stress must not be on athletic dominance, winning at any cost, or interest in one team's or country's desires and ambitions.

Athletes should be encouraged to make every effort to prove to everyone their desire and aim: competition with other nations of the world in an atmosphere of friendliness and good will. They should be encouraged to row, jump, and play to win, but at the same time their main objective should be to understand their fellow participants and the countries they represent. The end is not to break a world's record in athletic competition; rather, it is to establish a record for making friends. This spirit should be displayed in all athletic competition that is conducted on a year-to-year basis in various sports and other physical education activities. Only if this is true will sports be used as a medium for promoting international good will.

World seminars and conferences on sports should be held more often. Participants, representing many nations, will thus be able to sit down at the discussion table and—in an atmosphere of friendliness and cooperation—attempt to discover means by which the benefits derived from athletic programs may be extended to a greater portion of the world's population.

Sports have great potential, not only as a medium for enriching individual lives everywhere, but also as a force in promoting international good will and understanding among the peoples of the world. Physical educators should constantly be on the lookout for these opportunities. In this way it will be possible for the physical education profession to do its part in developing a "one world" era in which there will be no "iron curtains," no "cold" or "hot" wars, no atom or hydrogen bombs, no "brushfires"; rather, it will be a world in which people live side by side peacefully, cooperatively, and happily. As Sargent Shriver, Director of the Peace Corps, wrote in an article entitled, "The Moral Force of Sport," which appeared in an issue of *Sports Illustrated:*

> It is on the playing fields of Africa and Asia and Latin America that, in some measure, the battle for a free and peaceful community of nations will be won. The moral force and dedication of our overseas volunteers represent qualities shared by the great majority of American athletes—qualities which will [always] be with us. . . .

Bibliography

American Association for Health, Physical Education, and Recreation, *Physical Education: An Interpretation.* Washington, D.C.: The Association, 1952.

American Association for Health, Physical Education, and Recreation, *Physical Education for High School Students,* rev. ed. Washington, D.C.: The Association, 1960.

Anderson, Vivienne, and Daniel R. Davies, *Patterns of Educational Leadership.* Englewood Cliffs, N.J.: Prentice-Hall, Inc., 1956.

Bookwalter, Karl W., and Carolyn W. Bookwalter, (eds.), *Fitness for Secondary School Youth.* Washington, D.C.: American Association for Health, Physical Education, and Recreation, 1956.

Brown, Camille, and Rosalind Cassidy, *Theory in Physical Education: A Guide to Program Change.* Philadelphia: Lea & Febiger, 1963.

Bucher, Charles A., *Administration of School Health and Physical Education Programs,* 3rd. ed. St. Louis: The C. V. Mosby Company, 1963.

————, *Foundations of Physical Education,* 4th ed. St. Louis: The C. V. Mosby Company, 1964.

————, *et al., Methods and Materials for Secondary School Physical Education,* 2nd ed. St. Louis: The C. V. Mosby Company, 1965.

————, and Evelyn Reade, *Physical Education and Health in the Elementary School,* 2nd ed., New York: The Macmillan Company, 1964.

Cowell, Charles C., and Wellman L. France, *Philosophy and Principles of Physical Education.* Englewood Cliffs, N.J.: Prentice-Hall, Inc., 1963.

Division for Girls' and Women's Sports, *Special Events in the Girls' Sports Program.* Washington, D.C.: The American Association for Health, Physical Education, and Recreation, 1961.

Division for Girls' and Women's Sports, *Standards in Sports for Girls and Women.* Washington, D.C.: The American Association for Health, Physical Education, and Recreation, 1958.

Educational Policies Commission, *School Athletics, Problems, and Policies.* Washington, D.C.: National Education Association, 1954.

Esslinger, Arthur A., and Edward F. Voltmer, *The Organization and Administration of Physical Education,* 3rd. ed. New York: Appleton-Century-Crofts, Inc., 1958.

Forsythe, Charles E., *Administration of High School Athletics,* 4th ed. Englewood Cliffs, N.J.: Prentice-Hall, Inc., 1962.

————, *The Athletic Director's Handbook.* Englewood Cliffs, N.J.: Prentice-Hall, Inc., 1956.

Grieve, Andrew W., *Directing High School Athletics.* Englewood Cliffs, N.J.: Prentice-Hall, Inc., 1963.

Leavitt, Norma M., and Hartley D. Price, *Intramural and Recreational Sports,* 2nd ed. New York: The Ronald Press Company, 1958.

Leonard, Fred, and George Afflect, *A Guide to the History of Physical Education,* 3rd ed. Philadelphia: Lea & Febiger, 1947.

Rice, Emmett A., *et al., A Brief History of Physical Education,* 4th ed. New York: The Ronald Press Company, 1958.

Scott, Harry A., *Competitive Sports in Schools and Colleges.* New York: Harper & Row, Publishers, 1951.

Van Dalen, Deobold B., *et al., A World History of Physical Education.* Englewood Cliffs, N.J.: Prentice-Hall, Inc., 1953.

Index

Index